the Young

DACIA

N

EUXINE SEA

GREATER
ARMENIA

PONTUS

MACEDONIA THRACE

BITHYNIA

Thessalonica
Philippi

Beroea

Troas

GALATIA

CAPPADOCIA

PHRYGIA

Antioch of Pisidia

Lystra
Derbe

Tarsus

PARTHIAN

Ephesus
Laodicea

Colossae

CILICIA

Antioch

SYRIA

KINGDOM

Athens

Corinth
Cenchrea

LYCIA

CYPRUS

PHOENICIA

Sidon
Tyre

Damascus

GALILEE

CRETE

Caesarea
Joppa
Gaza

JUDAEA

Jerusalem

EAN SEA

Cyrene

CYRENAICA

Alexandria

IDUMAEA

ARABIA

N

MT.
SINAI

EGYPT

RED SEA

THE YOUNG CHURCH
IN ACTION

By J. B. PHILLIPS

THE GOSPELS *translated into Modern English*

THE YOUNG CHURCH IN ACTION
A translation of The Acts of the Apostles

LETTERS TO YOUNG CHURCHES
A translation of the New Testament Epistles

YOUR GOD IS TOO SMALL

MAKING MEN WHOLE

PLAIN CHRISTIANITY *and other broadcast talks*

APPOINTMENT WITH GOD

THE YOUNG CHURCH
IN ACTION

A translation of
The Acts of the Apostles

by
J. B. PHILLIPS

New York
THE MACMILLAN COMPANY
1955

To the Men's Study Group of St. John's, Red-hill, Surrey, whose uninhibited comments greatly helped me to translate this remarkable book.

TRANSLATOR'S PREFACE

IT IS impossible to spend several months in close study of the remarkable short book, conventionally known as the Acts of the Apostles, without being profoundly stirred and, to be honest, disturbed. The reader is stirred because he is seeing Christianity, the real thing, in action for the first time in human history. The newborn Church, as vulnerable as any human child, having neither money, influence nor power in the ordinary sense, is setting forth joyfully and courageously to win the pagan world for God through Christ. The young Church, like all young creatures, is appealing in its simplicity and singleheartedness. Here we are seeing the Church in its first youth, valiant and unspoiled—a body of ordinary men and women joined in an unconquerable fellowship never before seen on this earth.

Yet we cannot help feeling disturbed as well as moved, for this surely is the Church as it was meant to be. It is vigorous and flexible, for these are the days before it ever became fat and short of breath through prosperity, or muscle-bound by overorganization. These men did not make "acts of faith," they believed; they did not "say their prayers," they really prayed. They did not hold conferences on psychosomatic medicine, they simply healed the sick. But if they were uncomplicated and naïve by modern standards, we have ruefully to admit that they were open on the God-ward side in a way that is almost unknown today.

No one can read this book without being convinced that there is Someone here at work besides mere human beings. Perhaps because of their very simplicity, perhaps because of their readiness to believe, to obey, to give, to suffer, and if need be to die, the Spirit of God found what surely He must always be seeking—a fellowship of men and women so united in love and faith that He can work in them and through them with the minimum of let or hindrance. Consequently it is a matter of sober historical fact that never before has any small body of ordinary people so moved the world that their enemies could say, with tears of rage in their eyes, that these men "have turned the world upside down"! (17, 6)

In the pages of this unpretentious second book, written by the author of the third Gospel, the fresh air of Heaven is plainly blowing, and to turn from the vitality of these pages to almost any current Christian writing, be it a theological book or a Church periodical, is to bring tears to Christian eyes. Of course the moment one suggests that our tragically divided and tradition-choked Church might learn from this early unsophistication one is accused of oversimplification of the issues involved in our modern world. But it should be remembered that the ancient world was not without its complex problems also. It is of course possible that the translator has had his head turned by too close a study of these artless and energetic pages, but nevertheless he feels after such study that the Holy Spirit has a way of short-circuiting human problems. Indeed, in exactly the same way as Jesus Christ in the flesh cut right through the matted layers of tradition and exposed the real issue; just as He again and again brought down a theoretical problem to a personal issue, so we find here the Spirit of Jesus dealing not so much with problems as with people. Many problems comparable to modern complexities never arise here because the men and women concerned were of one heart and mind in the Spirit. Many another issue is never allowed to arise because these early Christians were led by the Spirit to the main task of bringing people to God through Christ and were not permitted to enjoy fascinating sidetracks. One can hardly avoid concluding, since God's Holy Spirit cannot conceivably have changed one iota through the centuries, that He is perfectly prepared to short-circuit, by an inflow of love, wisdom and understanding, many human problems today. The trouble is that there is nothing quite so effective as a defense against the invasion of the Spirit as a good knotty modern problem. We need, for instance, do nothing about securing a united Church so long as we have convinced ourselves and our fellows that such a thing is impossible, at any rate within measurable time—which simultaneously "passes the buck" to our children or grandchildren and safeguards the inviolability of our own denomination. If it were not for the strong insulation, so powerfully built up and so tenaciously held by so many people, there can be little doubt but that a new Pentecost would quickly sweep away our differences to the limbo where they belong.

There are two types of people especially who should read and study this book. First, those intellectuals who assume that Christianity was founded on a myth and is in any case a spent force today. For this book of Luke's, whose authenticity no reputable scholar disputes, takes more than a little explaining away. This is the beginning of the Christian era. This is the beginning of the practice of those virtues which scientific humanists so frequently assume to be natural to all human beings everywhere, despite the evidence of two world wars and the observable values of atheistic Communism.

The second group of people who should certainly study this book with the closest attention are what we might call the churchy-minded. They will find in this honest account of the early Church a corroboration of what Jesus meant when He said, "The wind bloweth where it listeth, and thou hearest the sound thereof, but canst not tell whence it cometh, and whither it goeth: so is every one that is born of the Spirit." For this is the story of Spirit-directed activities and there is what appears to be from the human point of view an arbitrariness, even a capriciousness, in the operation of the Holy Spirit. Of course from the real point of view God's work is neither arbitrary nor capricious—and this will be plain to us one day. Yet it will often appear to be so in the present human set-up, for God's wisdom is working at a different level from our own. When we compare the strength and vigor of the Spirit-filled early Church with the confused and sometimes feeble performance of the Church today, we might perhaps conclude that when man's rigidity attempts to canalize the free and flexible flow of the Spirit he is left to his own devices.

It is one of the curious phenomena of modern times that it is considered perfectly respectable to be abysmally ignorant of the Christian Faith. Men and women who would be deeply ashamed of having their ignorance exposed in matters of poetry, music, or painting, for example, are not in the least perturbed to be found ignorant of the New Testament. Indeed it is perfectly obvious from the remarks sometimes made by intellectuals and from their own writings, that apart from half-remembered scraps left over from childhood's memory they have no knowledge of the New Testament at all. Very very rarely does a man or woman give honest intelligent adult attention to the writings of the New

Testament and then decide that Jesus was merely a misguided man. Even less frequently will he conclude that the whole Christian religion is founded upon a myth. The plain fact is not that men have given the New Testament their serious attention and found it spurious, but that they have never given it their serious attention at all. Let our intelligent men and women be urged, goaded, even shamed into reading this remarkable collection of early Christian literature for themselves. Let this ignorance of what Christianity teaches and practices be shown up for the intellectual affectation that it really is. Let the ill informed critic of the Christian religion read particularly the Acts of the Apostles. Here is a simple, unvarnished, conscientious account of the behavior and actions of quite a small group of people who honestly believed that Jesus was right in His claims. Let the critics put aside for a moment their contempt for (and ignorance of) the Church as it is today, and let them feel afresh the astonishing impact of this tiny group of devoted men and women. Or let them read the letters of this same New Testament and see for themselves the new qualities of living which are taken almost as a matter of course in those human unselfconscious writings. No honest reader can evade the conclusion that something very powerful and very unusual has happened. People are unquestionably being changed at the root of their being: cowards become heroes; sinners are transformed; fear, greed, envy and pride are expelled by a flood of something above and beyond normal human experience. For in the pages of this New Testament the cruel, the wicked, the evil-minded and the God-less become filled with selfless love, with gay and generous courage. The critics of Christianity have got somehow to explain this. Moreover, within a couple of generations, or even less, the Message of Christ was being taken by devoted men and women to a good part of the then known world. The new fellowship of those who knew God through Christ proved highly infectious and groups of "brothers" (which, it must be pointed out, included "sisters") sprang up and flourished in the most unlikely places.

Now let us freely admit that there is much in the Church's history of which all Christians must be bitterly ashamed. No one could be proud of the historical fact of such a thing as the two rival Popes cursing each other from their head-quarters in Rome and Constantinople! No one is proud of religious wars or persecutions. No one is proud of that pious hypocrisy which could affect to care for men's souls while not being in the least concerned for their physical or social welfare. And no one worthy of the name of Christian is proud of a divided and largely ineffectual Church. Yet for all its glaring faults there are not lacking in the Church today thousands of men and women with precisely the same devotion to Christ as the early Christians so powerfully exhibited. Thousands today are being persecuted for their faith, thousands are suffering "the loss of all things" with the same unadvertised courage as did the Christians of the early centuries. Of course this is quite unknown to our in-tellectual who has most certainly never read of the present-day activities of the world-wide Church. The Church has no trumpeter, and unless a missionary is captured by bandits or a Church leader tortured by Communists, or, what is even better "copy," a minister of the Church "goes wrong," little place in the popular press is found for the activities of the living agents of the Holy Spirit today. But if the truth were told and a present-day Acts of the Apostles could be writ-ten—and read—many people would be astonished to learn of the extent and the effect of the work of today's Christians.

The secular history of the period covered by this book of the New Testament, for example, is of little importance com-pared with the spiritual history which is recorded, although of course at the time exactly the reverse must have appeared to be the case. (To the average Roman what could be less important than the ups-and-downs of a tiny sect who still followed the dead carpenter-preacher?) Yet the history told by Luke, fragmentary though it is, is the *real* history. The work done by the Holy Spirit through men and women is not only more important in the eyes of Heaven, but actu-ally has a far more lasting influence on human affairs than that of any secular authority. It is perfectly possible that the unpublicized and almost unknown activities of the Spirit through His human agents today are of more permanent importance than all the news recorded in the whole of the popular press.

Now the words written above must not be taken to mean

that the Spirit of God is at work solely through His conscious agents. It can scarcely be emphasized too strongly that to the early Christians who were all Jews (or at least Gentile converts to Judaism) it was a profound shock to discover that God not only included Gentiles in His plan of salvation, but that by His Spirit He was actually at work in the hearts of Gentiles before the Gospel arrived. Peter's words, "Of a truth I perceive that God is no respecter of persons" (10, 34), were far more revolutionary than they sound to us today. Yet members of the fellowship of the early Church appear to have been the necessary agents between men seeking God and God Himself. The Ethiopian eunuch, for example, was indeed seeking God, but the agency of Philip was necessary before he could find Him (8, 27). Cornelius, to whom we shall refer again later, receives one of the highest commendations ever given in the New Testament to a non-Christian. But it needed the agency of Peter to bring him to a fuller knowledge of the Truth as it is in Christ (10, 25). The men of Macedonia were seeking after God, but it needed the faith and courage of Paul to bring the Gospel across to them in Europe (16, 9). Apollos knew the Old Testament well, but had apparently got no further than the baptism of John (18, 24, 25). It needed the agency of Aquila and Priscilla to lead him on into the Christian knowledge of God. In short, we might fairly say that although this book shows the Holy Spirit to be at work in the hearts of men who are not yet Christians the same Spirit uses members of the living Church to bring them into Christian certainty about God. And this is a situation which has innumerable parallels today.

Now important as the book is for the critic of Christianity to study, it is just as important for the modern Christian, especially, as I have said above, for the churchy-minded. For if "love laughs at locksmiths," divine Love certainly is completely unrestrained by the prejudices and timid rigidities of man. Appropriately enough God comes upon the scene with the sound of "a rushing mighty wind," and it is with the wholesome gustiness of a boisterous wind that the deep-seated prejudices and limited ideas of man are blown sky-high. Humanly speaking the Christian Faith might easily have become a little Jewish sect if it had not been for the powerful Wind of Heaven. As we read we may find that this celestial gale blows away some of our own prejudices and preferences. Indeed we may find that we are far more indoctrinated by the tenets of our own particular denomination than we knew. There are many with us who insist that the Holy Spirit can only be given through the orthodox channels, by which they usually mean the channels of their own particular Church. Doubtless God is a God of order, but at Caesarea, while Peter was still preaching, the Holy Spirit was given unmistakably to pagans who had not yet been baptized, let alone confirmed! (10, 44) Again, there are those who would hedge around the rite of baptism and only after very careful preparation would they baptize anyone. Yet Paul, apparently with no misgivings, and certainly with little chance of proper preparation, baptizes the Philippian jailer *and his whole household* in the small hours of the morning! (16, 33) What are we to conclude? Not of course that God prefers irregularity to order, but that His Spirit is quite capable of dispensing with rules or regulations if the occasion demands it, *and that we must never deny this possibility*.

I would warmly commend to every modern evangelist a study of the actual Message proclaimed by the young Church. The call of the Good News was not the emphasis on man's sinfulness, but that the Man Jesus Whom many of them had known personally was no less than God's Chosen One. Through this Man Jesus God had made Himself personally known; the proof that the Man Jesus was God's Christ was the Resurrection, a shining fact to which many of them were eyewitnesses; the Good News was that if men would turn from their former ways and accept the forgiveness of God through Christ, then the Spirit of God was living and available to enter their hearts and transform them. Those who so accepted the fact that God had become Man in Christ were "followers of the Way," and since they now shared the truest human loyalty they enjoyed the deepest possible fellowship.

Now in much modern evangelism the main plank of the platform is the emphasis, again and again, upon the utter sinfulness of man. "The Bible says, 'all have sinned,'" the modern evangelist will shout. "The Bible says, 'There is none righteous, no not one.' The Bible says, 'All our righteousnesses are as filthy rags.'" But is not this book a legitimate

xiv   TRANSLATOR'S PREFACE

part of the Bible? Luke, knowing nothing of this emphasis
on man's depravity, says quite simply of the unconverted
Cornelius that he was "a devout man, and one that feared God
. . . , which gave much alms to the people, and prayed to
God alway" (10, 2). He further records that no less a per-
sonage than the angel of the Lord assures him that "thy
prayers and thine alms are come up for a memorial before
God" (10, 4). (This statement might be compared with
Article 13 from the Anglican Prayer Book.) What is even
more surprising is to find Peter, blurting out the truth as he
suddenly saw it, "Of a truth I perceive that God is no respecter of persons: *But in every nation he that feareth Him,
and worketh righteousness, is accepted with Him*" (10, 34–
35). Indeed, the modern technique of arousing guilt by quoting isolated texts of Scripture is not found in this book at all.
Naturally enough when the Truth was proclaimed to the
Jews, as on the Day of Pentecost, they were "pricked to the
heart," for as a race they were responsible not only for the
rejection, but for the public execution, of God's Christ. But
we do not read of any similar reaction when the Gospel is
preached to the Gentiles.

There are other shocks for us. There are those who make
much of the Greek word *ekklēsia* (from the Greek words *ek*,
meaning "out of," and *kalein*, "to call") and claim that from
the earliest times the Church was conscious of being such,
that is, "a called-out people." But Luke is plainly unaware of
the word's significance, for though he uses *ekklēsia* to de-
scribe the early Church he uses precisely the same word
when the town clerk dismisses the crowd after the riot in
Ephesus! (19, 41) If the word had already secured a special
meaning we can hardly imagine Luke so far forgetting himself as to use it for an excited crowd of pagans!

There are Christians who make exaggerated claims for the
primacy of Peter and even claim, without the slightest historical evidence, that he was the first Bishop of Rome! But here
in this book, in spite of Peter's claim that it would be by his
mouth that the Gentiles would hear the word of the Gospel
and believe (15, 7), it becomes increasingly plain that Paul is
God's chosen instrument for this purpose, and that in spite of
a highly irregular ordination!

Perhaps we are not supposed to speculate, but one cannot

help wondering why there is no mention of the incident which Paul recorded in Galatians 2, 11 ff. and where it fits into this story. It was indeed a crucial moment for the Church. Peter, it will be recalled, unhappily exhibiting that same fear of other people's opinion which led him to deny his Master, was refusing to eat his meals with the Gentile Christians. Paul immediately saw what was at stake and publicly condemned Peter's action. Since Luke was such a close associate of Paul's it is a remarkable thing that no mention is made of this momentous reprimand. But perhaps by now it did not greatly matter since Paul had most thoroughly demonstrated that the Gospel, and indeed all the riches of God, were to be shared by all who believed, whether Jew, Gentile, bond or free. We do not know whether it was the tact of Luke or the charity of Paul which led to the omission of this incident in the history of the young Church; nevertheless it must not be lost sight of in the study of these early significant days.

A further point is worth noting. Throughout the book the main enemies of the Church's life, as in the life of Christ Himself, were the entrenched self-righteous—in this case the Jews. The persecution by non-Christians was spasmodic and more than once designed to please the Jews. But all the bitter relentless campaign of persecution and misrepresentation, particularly of Paul, must be laid at the door of the Jews. Christ said that "Yea, the time cometh when whosoever killeth you will think that he doeth God service." He knew and foresaw that the bitterest enemies of those who knew God would be those who only thought they did—and that is a situation which has not changed with the centuries.

Finally, whatever conclusions our modern conferences may reach, there can be no reasonable doubt but that the early Church possessed the power to heal and even to raise the dead. Luke was a careful writer as well as a medical man himself and is not likely to have exaggerated such happenings. Even though he may have had to rely on the evidence of others for those early days when, for example, the young Church exercised a healing ministry in the Temple, he himself was actually present with Paul when they were shipwrecked on the island of Malta. Yet he records almost as a matter of routine that after Paul's initial success with the

Governor's father, many other sick people on the island were healed at his hands. That the Church today has very largely lost this power of healing the sick is undeniable, although it is heartening to know that in recent years Christians all over the world are not content to accept this loss as the inevitable price we must pay for the march of Science. But we cannot help looking wistfully at the sheer spiritual power of the minute young Church, which was expressed not only by healing the body but "by many signs and wonders" which amply demonstrated the fact that these men were in close touch with God.

Of course it is easy to "write off" this little history of the Church's first beginnings as simply an account of an enthusiastic but ill regulated and unorganized adolescence, to be followed by a well disciplined maturity in which embarrassing irregularities no longer appear. But that is surely too easy an explanation altogether. We in the modern Church have unquestionably *lost* something. Whether it is due to the atrophy of the quality which the New Testament calls "faith," whether it is due to a stifling churchiness, whether it is due to our sinful complacency over the scandal of a divided Church, or whatever the cause may be, very little of the modern Church could bear comparison with the spiritual drive, the genuine fellowship, and the gay unconquerable courage of the Young Church.

REDHILL, 1954/

SWANAGE, 1955.   J. B. PHILLIPS

THE ACTS OF
THE APOSTLES

"*The Acts of the Apostles*," *which is the conventional title
of this remarkable book, is something of a mistranslation.
The Greek title,* Praxeis Apostolōn, *has no definite articles
and could be translated more accurately "Acts of Apostles,"
or, quite fairly, "Some Acts of Some Apostles." The author,
who is unquestionably Luke, makes no attempt to give an exhaustive history of the early days of the Church—much as
we may wish he had done so—but he does record with vivid-
ness and accuracy some actions of some Apostles.*

*The book is characterized by the same easy-flowing Greek
as the third Gospel, its vocabulary containing some fifty words
common to these two works, but not found elsewhere in the
New Testament. As in his Gospel, Luke shows the same deep
interest in women, the same sympathy for the sick and poor,
and the same concern for the Gentiles. There is also the same
doctor's precision in the use of medical language.*

*Luke's sources of information were probably excellent. The
deacon Philip was still living at Caesarea during the two years
of Paul's captivity at Rome with which this book closes, and
Luke would have been able to obtain much early information from him. There would also have been many still living
who were present on the Day of Pentecost and who would
have supplied information about those early days. In the latter
part of the book Luke is obviously making use of his own
personal diaries. The first person plural is used quite naturally
(16, 10–17; 20, 5 to 21, 18; 27, 1 to 28, 16), and the narrative
gains in dramatic power through the reader's sudden realiza-
tion that the author was actually present at the time. Indeed,
Luke's close association with Paul, an association which meant
sharing a good deal of the latter's dangers and fatigues, is not
the least of Luke's qualifications as author of a book such as*

1

this. It is rash to surmise, but humanly speaking, the Gospel for all men might easily have been confined to Jews and Gentile proselytes if it had not been for the vision, courage and tenacity of Paul.

The period covered by this book is roughly from 30 to 63, that is, from the Ascension of Christ to Paul's imprisonment at Rome. It is a fascinating guess, though no more than a guess, that Luke intended to write a third work, for the present book ends on a triumphant but rather unfinished note. Possibly Luke was never able to complete the story, possibly the work never got beyond the notes of events which he almost certainly took, possibly the work was irretrievably lost. Or, of course, the existence of such a work may be a wild guess with no foundation at all. Nevertheless readers of this book may feel, as I do, not only a hunger for more, but a sense that the author had not fully finished the history he set out to write.

Luke is a careful historian and his geographical as well as his historical accuracy should be noted. He has a sound knowledge of Roman government and procedure. Although it cannot be proved, there is at least a likelihood that he was a Greek-speaking Gentile, converted under the ministry of Paul and Barnabas at Antioch.

It is most difficult to assign a date to this work. Some incline to the belief that it was written shortly after the closing date mentioned in the book, which would put it as early as 65. Others are convinced that it was written after the fall of Jerusalem (70), and others again consider that Luke must have had access to the book by the Jewish historian Josephus, Jewish Antiquities, which did not appear till about 94. When I translated the Gospels in 1952 I gave the date of Luke's Gospel as about 80, but after close study of this second volume from Luke's pen, I am inclined to place the date of its writing not very long after Paul's two-year imprisonment, possibly about 65. If I am now right, then the Gospel naturally was written before the present work, though not necessarily very long before.

INTRODUCTION

My dear Theophilus,   1

In my first book I gave you some account of all that Jesus   1
began to do and teach until the time of His Ascension. Before
He ascended He gave His instructions, through the Holy
Spirit, to the Special Messengers of His choice. For after His
suffering He showed Himself alive to them in many convincing ways, and appeared to them repeatedly over a period
of forty days talking with them about the affairs of the Kingdom of God.

JESUS' PARTING WORDS BEFORE HIS ASCENSION

On one occasion, while He was eating a meal with them,   1
He emphasized that they were not to leave Jerusalem, but to   4
wait for the Father's Promise.

"You have already heard Me speak about this," He said,
"for John used to baptize with water, but before many days
are passed you will be baptized with the Holy Spirit."

This naturally brought them all together, and they asked
Him,

"Lord, is this the time when You are going to restore the
Kingdom to Israel?"

To this He replied,

"You cannot know times and dates which have been fixed
by the Father's sole Authority. But you are to be given
power when the Holy Spirit has come to you. You will be
witnesses to Me, not only in Jerusalem, not only throughout
Judaea, not only in Samaria, but to the very ends of the
earth!"

When He had said these words He was lifted up before
their eyes till a cloud hid Him from their sight. While they
were still gazing up into the sky as He went, suddenly two
men dressed in white stood beside them and said,

"Men of Galilee, why are you standing here looking up
into the sky? This very Jesus Who has been taken up from
you into Heaven will come back in just the same way as you
have seen Him go."

At this they returned to Jerusalem from the Mount of
Olives which is near the city, only a sabbath day's journey
away. On entering Jerusalem they went straight to the up-

stairs room where they had been staying. There were Peter, John, James, Andrew, Philip, Thomas, Bartholomew, Matthew, James the son of Alphaeus, Simon the Patriot, and Judas the son of James. By common consent all these men, together with the women who had followed Jesus, Mary His Mother, as well as His brothers, devoted themselves to prayer.

JUDAS' PLACE IS FILLED

1
15
It was during this period that Peter stood up among the brothers—there were about a hundred and twenty present at the time—and said,

"My brothers, the prophecy of Scripture given through the Holy Spirit by the lips of David concerning Judas was bound to come true. He was the man who acted as guide to those who arrested Jesus, though he was one of our number and he had a share in this ministry of ours."

(This man had bought a piece of land with the proceeds of his infamy, but his body swelled up and his intestines burst. This fact became well known to all the residents of Jerusalem so that the piece of land came to be called in their language Akeldama, which means "the bloody field.")

"Now it is written in the book of Psalms of such a man:

Let his habitation be made desolate,
And let no man dwell therein:

and

His office let another take.

"It becomes necessary then that whoever joins us must be someone who has been in our company during the whole time that the Lord Jesus lived His life with us, from the beginning when John baptized Him until the day when He was taken up from us. This man must be an eyewitness with us to the Resurrection of Jesus."

Two men were put forward, Joseph called Barsabas who was also called Justus, and Matthias. Then they prayed,

"Thou, Lord, Who knowest the hearts of all men, show us which of these two Thou hast chosen to accept that apostle's ministry which Judas forfeited to go where he belonged."

Then they drew lots for these men, and the lot fell to

Matthias, and thereafter he was considered equally an Apostle
with the Eleven.

THE FIRST PENTECOST FOR THE YOUNG CHURCH

Then when the actual Day of Pentecost came they were   2
all assembled together. Suddenly there was a sound from   1
heaven like the rushing of a violent wind, and it filled the
whole house where they were seated. Before their eyes appeared tongues like flames, which separated off and settled
above the head of each one of them. They were all filled with
the Holy Spirit and began to speak in different languages as
the Spirit gave them power to proclaim His Message.

THE CHURCH'S FIRST IMPACT ON DEVOUT JEWS

Now there were staying in Jerusalem Jews of deep faith   2
from every nation of the world. When they heard this sound   5
a crowd quickly collected and were completely bewildered
because each one of them heard these men speaking in his own
language. They were absolutely amazed and said in their
astonishment,

"Listen, surely all these speakers are Galileans? Then how
does it happen that every single one of us can hear the particular language he has known from a child? There are Parthians,
Medes and Elamites; there are men whose homes are in
Mesopotamia, in Judaea and Cappadocia, Pontus, Asia,
Phrygia, Pamphylia, Egypt, and the parts of Africa near
Cyrene, as well as visitors from Rome! There are Jews and
proselytes, men from Crete and men from Arabia, yet we can
all hear these men speaking of the magnificence of God in our
native language."

Everyone was utterly amazed and did not know what to
make of it. Indeed they kept saying to each other,

"What on earth can this mean?"

But there were others who laughed mockingly and said,

"These fellows have drunk too much new wine!"

PETER EXPLAINS THE FULFILLMENT OF GOD'S PROMISE

Then Peter, with the Eleven standing by him, raised his   2
voice and addressed them: *   14

* For an expanded version of this address, see Appendix, pages 82–86.

"Fellow Jews, and all who are living now in Jerusalem, listen carefully to what I say while I explain to you what has happened! These men are not drunk as you suppose—it is after all only nine o'clock in the morning of this great Feast day. No, this is something which was predicted by the prophet Joel,

And it shall be in the last days, saith God,
I will pour forth of my Spirit upon all flesh:
And your sons and your daughters shall prophesy,
And your young men shall see visions,
And your old men shall dream dreams:
Yea and on my servants and on my handmaidens in those
    days
Will I pour forth of my Spirit; and they shall prophesy.
And I will shew wonders in the heaven above,
And signs on the earth beneath;
Blood, and fire, and vapor of smoke:
The sun shall be turned into darkness,
And the moon into blood,
Before the day of the Lord come,
That great and notable *day:*
And it shall be, that whosoever shall call on the name of
    the Lord shall be saved.

"Men of Israel, I beg you to listen to my words. Jesus of Nazareth was a man proved to you by God Himself through the works of power, the miracles and the signs which God showed through Him here amongst you—as you very well know. This Man, Who was put into your power by the predetermined Plan and foreknowledge of God, you nailed up and murdered, and you used for your purpose men without the Law! But God would not allow the bitter pains of death to touch Him. He raised Him to life again—and indeed there was nothing by which death could hold such a Man. When David speaks about Him he says,

I beheld the Lord always before my face;
For he is on my right hand, that I should not be moved:
Therefore my heart was glad, and my tongue rejoiced;
Moreover my flesh also shall dwell in hope:

Because thou wilt not leave my soul in Hades,
Neither wilt thou give thy Holy One to see corruption.
Thou madest known unto me the ways of life;
Thou shalt make me full of gladness with thy countenance.

"Men and brother Jews, I can surely speak freely to you
about the Patriarch David. There is no doubt that he died
and was buried, and his grave is here among us to this day.
But while he was alive he was a prophet. He knew that God
had given him a most solemn Promise that He would place
one of his descendants upon His throne. He foresaw the
Resurrection of Christ, and it is this of which he is speaking.
Christ was not deserted in death and His body was never
destroyed. *Christ is the Man Jesus, Whom God raised up—
a fact of which all of us are eyewitnesses!* He has been raised
to the right hand of God; He has received from His Father
and poured out upon us the promised Holy Spirit—*that* is
what you now see and hear! David never ascended to Heaven,
but he certainly said,

The Lord said unto my *Lord,*
Sit thou on my right hand,
Till I make thine enemies the footstool of thy feet.

"Now therefore the whole nation of Israel must know
beyond the shadow of a doubt that this Jesus, Whom you
crucified, God has declared to be both Lord and Christ."

THE REACTION TO PETER'S SPEECH

When they heard this they were cut to the quick, and they   2
cried to Peter and the other Apostles,   37
"Men and fellow Jews, what shall we do now?"
Peter told them,
"You must repent and every one of you must be baptized
in the Name of Jesus Christ, so that you may have your sins
forgiven and receive the gift of the Holy Spirit. For it is to
you and your children that this great Message comes. Yes,
and to all who are far away, to as many as the Lord our God
shall call to Himself!"
Peter said much more than this as he gave his testimony
and implored them, saying,
"Save yourselves from this perverted generation!"

THE FIRST LARGE-SCALE CONVERSION

2   Then those who welcomed his message were baptized, and
41 on that day alone about three thousand souls were added to
the number of disciples. They continued steadily learning the
teaching of the Apostles, and joined in their fellowship, in
the breaking of bread, and in prayer.

Everyone felt a deep sense of awe while many miracles and
signs took place through the Apostles. All the believers shared
everything in common; they sold their possessions and goods
and divided the proceeds among the fellowship according to
individual need. Day after day they met by common consent
in the Temple; they broke bread together in their homes, sharing meals with simple joy. They praised God continually and
all the people respected them. Every day the Lord added to
their number those who were finding salvation.

A PUBLIC MIRACLE AND ITS EXPLANATION

3   One afternoon Peter and John were on their way to the
1   Temple for the three o'clock hour of prayer. A man who had
been lame from birth was being carried along in the crowd,
for it was the daily practice to put him down at what was
known as the Beautiful Gate of the Temple, so that he could
beg from the people as they went in. As this man saw Peter
and John just about to enter he asked them to give him something. Peter looked straight at the man and so did John. Then
Peter said,

"Look straight at us!"

The man looked at them expectantly, hoping that they
would give him something.

"If you are expecting silver or gold," Peter said to him,
"I have neither, but what I have I will certainly give you.
In the Name of Jesus Christ of Nazareth, *get up and walk!*"

Then he took him by the right hand and helped him up. At
once his feet and ankle bones were strengthened, and he
positively jumped to his feet, stood, and then walked. Then he
went with them into the Temple, where he walked about,
leaping and praising God. Everyone noticed him as he walked
and praised God and recognized him as the same beggar who
used to sit at the Beautiful Gate, and they were all overcome
with wonder and sheer astonishment at what had happened

to him. Then while the man himself still clung to Peter and John all the people in their excitement ran together and crowded round them in Solomon's Porch. When Peter saw this he spoke to the crowd,

"Men of Israel, why are you so surprised at this, and why are you staring at us as though we had made this man walk through some power or piety of our own? It is the God of Abraham and Isaac and Jacob, the God of our fathers, Who has done this thing to honor His Servant Jesus—the Man Whom you betrayed and denied in the presence of Pilate, even when he had decided to let Him go. But you disowned the Holy and Righteous One, and begged to be granted instead a man who was a murderer! You killed the Prince of Life, but God raised Him from the dead—a fact of which we are eyewitnesses. It is the Name of this same Jesus, it is faith in that Name, which has cured this man whom you see and recognize. Yes, it was faith in Christ which gave this man perfect health and strength in full view of you all.

"Now of course I know, my brothers, that you had no idea what you were doing any more than your leaders had. But God had foretold through all His prophets that His Christ must suffer and this was how His words came true. Now you must repent and turn to God so that your sins may be wiped out, that time after time your souls may know the refreshment that comes from the Presence of God. Then He will send you Jesus, your long-heralded Christ, although for the time He must remain in Heaven until that universal Restoration of which God spoke in ancient times through all His Holy Prophets. For Moses said, 3
17

A prophet shall the Lord God raise up unto you from among your brethren, like unto me; to him shall ye hearken in all things whatsoever he shall speak unto you. And it shall be that every soul, which shall not hearken to that prophet, shall be utterly destroyed from among the people.

Indeed, all the prophets from Samuel onwards who have spoken at all have foretold these days. You are the sons of the prophets and heirs of the Agreement which God made with our fathers when He said to Abraham, 'Through your children shall all the families of the earth be blessed.' It was to you first

that God sent His Servant after He had raised Him from the
dead, to bring you great blessing by turning every one of you
away from his evil ways."

THE FIRST CLASH WITH JEWISH AUTHORITIES

4
1   While they were still talking to the people the priests, the
     captain of the Temple Guard and the Sadducees moved
toward them, thoroughly incensed that they should be teaching the people and should inform them that in the case of Jesus
there had been a resurrection from the dead. So they arrested
them and, since it was now evening, kept them in custody
until the next day. Nevertheless, many of those who had
heard what they said believed, and the number of men alone
rose to about five thousand.

PETER'S BOLDNESS EMBARRASSES THE AUTHORITIES

4
5   Next day the leading members of the Council, the elders
     and scribes met in Jerusalem with Annas the High Priest,
Caiaphas, John, Alexander, and the whole of the High Priest's
family. They had the Apostles brought in to stand before
them and they asked them formally,
    "By what power and in whose name have you done this
thing?"
    At this Peter, filled with the Holy Spirit, spoke to them,
    "Leaders of the people and elders, if we are being called in
question today over the matter of a kindness done to a helpless man and as to how he was healed, it is high time that all
of you and the whole people of Israel knew that it was done
in the Name of Jesus Christ of Nazareth! He is the One
Whom you crucified but Whom God raised from the dead,
and it is by His power that this man at our side stands in
your presence perfectly well. He is the 'Stone which you
builders rejected, which has now become the Head of the
corner.' In no one else can salvation be found. For in all the
world no other Name has been given to men but this, and
it is by this Name that we must be saved!"

4
13   When they saw the complete assurance of Peter and John,
     who were obviously uneducated and untrained men, they were
staggered. They recognized them as men who had been with
Jesus, yet since they could see the man who had been cured
standing beside them, they could find no effective reply. All

they could do was to order them out of the Sanhedrin and
hold a conference among themselves.

"What are we going to do with these men?" they said to
each other. "It is evident to everyone living in Jerusalem that
an extraordinary miracle has taken place through them, and
that is something we cannot deny. Nevertheless, to prevent
such a thing spreading further among the people, let us warn
them that if they say anything more to anyone in this Name
it will be at their peril."

So they called them in and ordered them bluntly not to
speak or teach a single further word about the Name of Jesus.
But Peter and John gave them this reply:

"Whether it is right in the eyes of God for us to listen to
what you say rather than to what He says, you must decide;
for we cannot help speaking about what we have actually
seen and heard!"

After further threats they let them go. They could not   4
think of any way of punishing them because of the attitude   21
of the people. Everybody was thanking God for what had
happened—that this miracle of healing had taken place in a
man who was more than forty years old.

After their release the Apostles went back to their friends
and reported to them what the Chief Priests and elders had
said to them. When they heard it they raised their voices to
God in united prayer and said,

"Thou art the One Who hast made the heaven and the
earth, the sea and all that is in them. It was Thou Who didst
speak by the Holy Spirit through the lips of our forefather
David Thy servant in the words:

Why did the Gentiles rage,
And the peoples imagine vain things?
The kings of the earth set themselves in array,
And the rulers were gathered together,
Against the Lord, and against his Anointed:

For indeed in this city the rulers have gathered together
against Thy Holy Servant, Jesus, Thine Anointed—yes,
Herod and Pontius Pilate, the Gentiles and the peoples of
Israel have gathered together to carry out what Thine Hand
and Will had planned to happen. And now, O Lord, observe
their threats and give Thy servants courage to speak Thy

Word fearlessly, while Thou dost stretch out Thine Hand
to heal, and cause signs and wonders to be performed in the
Name of Thy Holy Servant Jesus."

When they had prayed their meeting-place was shaken,
they were all filled with the Holy Spirit and spoke the Word
of God fearlessly.

THE CLOSE FELLOWSHIP OF THE YOUNG CHURCH

4   Among the large number who had become believers there
32   was complete agreement of heart and soul. Not one of them
claimed any of his possessions as his own but everything was
common property to all. The Apostles continued to give
their witness to the Resurrection of the Lord Jesus with great
force, and a wonderful spirit of generosity pervaded the
whole fellowship. Indeed, there was not a single person in
need among them, for those who owned land or property
would sell it and bring the proceeds of the sales and place
it at the Apostles' feet. They distributed to each one according to his need.

GENEROSITY AND COVETOUSNESS

4   It was at this time that Barnabas (the name, meaning Son
36   of Comfort, given by the Apostles to Joseph, a Levite from
Cyprus) sold his farm and put the proceeds at the Apostles'
disposal.

But there was a man named Ananias who, with his wife
Sapphira, had sold a piece of property but, with her full
knowledge, reserved part of the price for himself. He brought
the remainder to put at the Apostles' disposal. But Peter said
to him,

"Ananias, why has Satan so filled your mind that you could
cheat the Holy Spirit and keep back for yourself part of the
price of the land? Before the land was sold it was yours, and
after the sale the disposal of the price you received was en-
tirely in your hands, wasn't it? Then whatever made you
think of such a thing as this? You have not lied to men, but to
God!"

As soon as Ananias heard these words he collapsed and
died. All who were within earshot were appalled at this
incident. The young men got to their feet and after wrapping
up his body carried him out and buried him.

About three hours later it happened that his wife came 5
in not knowing what had taken place. Peter spoke directly 7
to her,

"Tell me, did you sell your land for so much?"

"Yes," she replied, "that was it."

Then Peter said to her,

"How could you two have agreed to put the Spirit of the
Lord to such a test? Listen, you can hear the footsteps of
the men who have just buried your husband coming back
through the door, and they will carry you out as well!"

Immediately she collapsed at Peter's feet and died. When
the young men came into the room they found her a dead
woman, and they carried her out and buried her by the side
of her husband. At this happening a deep sense of awe swept
over the whole Church and indeed over all those who heard
about it.

THE YOUNG CHURCH TAKES ITS STAND IN THE TEMPLE—

By common consent they all used to meet now in 5
Solomon's Porch. But as far as the others were concerned no 12b
one dared to associate with them, even though their general
popularity was very great. Yet more and more believers in the
Lord joined them, both men and women in really large
numbers.

—AND MIRACULOUS POWER RADIATES FROM IT

Many signs and wonders were now happening among the 5
people through the Apostles' ministry.* In consequence 15
people would bring out their sick into the streets and lay them
down on stretchers or beds, so that as Peter came by at least
his shadow might fall upon some of them. In addition a large
crowd collected from the cities round about Jerusalem,
bringing with them their sick and all those who were suffering from evil spirits. And they were all cured.

FURIOUS OPPOSITION REDUCED TO IMPOTENCE

All this roused the High Priest and his allies the Sadducean 5
party, and in a fury of jealousy they had the Apostles ar- 17
rested and put into the common jail. But during the night an

---

* Transposing the first part of v. 12 to the beginning of v. 15, which
makes better sense.

angel of the Lord opened the prison doors and led them out, saying,

"Go and stand and speak in the Temple. Tell the people all about this new Life!"

After receiving these instructions they entered the Temple about daybreak, and began to teach. When the High Priest arrived he and his supporters summoned the Sanhedrin and indeed the whole senate of the people of Israel. Then he sent to the jail to have the Apostles brought in. But when the officers arrived at the prison they could not find them there. They came back and reported,

"We found the prison securely locked and the guards standing on duty at the doors, but when we opened up we found no one inside."

When the captain of the Temple Guard and the Chief Priests heard this report they were completely mystified at the Apostles' disappearance and wondered what further developments there would be. However, someone arrived and reported to them,

"Why, the men you put in jail are standing in the Temple teaching the people!"

Then the captain went out with his men and fetched them. They dared not use any violence however, for the people might have stoned them. So they brought them in and made them stand before the Sanhedrin. The High Priest called for an explanation.

"We gave you the strictest possible orders," he said to them, "not to give any teaching in this Name. And look what has happened—you have filled Jerusalem with your teaching, and what is more you are determined to fasten the guilt of that Man's death upon us!"

THE APOSTLES SPEAK THE UNPALATABLE TRUTH

5
29   Then Peter and the Apostles answered him,

"It is our duty to obey the orders of God rather than the orders of men. It was the God of our fathers Who raised up Jesus, Whom you murdered by hanging Him on a cross of wood. God has raised this Man to His own right hand as Prince and Savior, to bring repentance and the forgiveness of sins to Israel. What is more, we are witnesses to these matters, and so is the Holy Spirit which God gives to those who obey His commands."

CALM COUNSEL TEMPORARILY PREVAILS

When the members of the Council heard these words they   5
were so furious that they wanted to kill them. But one man   33
stood up in the Assembly, a Pharisee by the name of Gamaliel, a teacher of the Law who was held in great respect by the
people, and gave orders for the Apostles to be taken outside
for a few minutes. Then he addressed the Assembly:

"Men of Israel, be very careful of what you intend to do in
the case of these men! Remember that some time ago a man
called Theudas made himself conspicuous by claiming to be
someone or other, and he had a following of four hundred
men. He was killed, all his followers were dispersed, and the
movement came to nothing. Then later, in the days of the
Census, that man Judas from Galilee appeared and enticed
many of the people to follow him. But he too died and his
whole following melted away. My advice to you now therefore is to let these men alone; leave them to themselves.
For if this teaching or movement is merely human it will
collapse of its own accord. But if it should be from God you
cannot defeat them, and you might actually find yourselves to
be fighting against God!"

They accepted his advice and called in the Apostles. They
had them beaten and after commanding them not to speak
in the Name of Jesus they let them go. So the Apostles went
out from the presence of the Sanhedrin full of joy that they
had been considered worthy to bear humiliation for the sake
of the Name. Then day after day in the Temple and in
people's houses they continued to teach unceasingly and to
proclaim the Good News of Jesus Christ.

THE FIRST DEACONS ARE CHOSEN

About this time, when the number of disciples was con-   6
tinually increasing, the Greeks complained that in the daily   1
distribution of food the Hebrew widows were being given
preferential treatment. The Twelve summoned the whole
body of the disciples together, and said,

"It is not right that we should have to neglect preaching
the Word of God in order to look after the accounts. You,
our brothers, must look round and pick out from your number seven men of good reputation who are both practical
and spiritually-minded and we will put them in charge of this

matter. Then we shall devote ourselves wholeheartedly to prayer and the ministry of the Word."

This brief speech met with unanimous approval and they chose Stephen, a man full of faith and the Holy Spirit, Philip, Prochorus, Nicanor, Timon, Parmenas, and Nicolas of Antioch who had previously been a convert to the Jewish faith. They brought these men before the Apostles, and they, after prayer, laid their hands upon them.

So the Word of God gained more and more ground. The number of disciples in Jerusalem very greatly increased, while a considerable proportion of the priesthood accepted the Faith.

THE ATTACK ON THE NEW DEACON, STEPHEN

6
8   Stephen, full of grace and spiritual power, continued to perform miracles and remarkable signs among the people. However, members of a Jewish synagogue known as the Libertines, together with some from the synagogues of Cyrene and Alexandria, as well as some men from Cilicia and Asia, tried debating with Stephen, but found themselves quite unable to stand up against either his practical wisdom or the spiritual force with which he spoke. In desperation they bribed men to allege, "We have heard this man making blasphemous statements against Moses and against God." At the same time they worked on the feelings of the people, the elders and the scribes. Then they suddenly confronted Stephen, seized him and marched him off before the Sanhedrin. There they brought forward false witnesses to say, "This man's speeches are one long attack against this holy place and the Law. We have heard him say that Jesus of Nazareth will destroy this place and change the customs which Moses handed down to us." All who sat there in the Sanhedrin looked intently at Stephen, and as they looked his face appeared to them like the face of an angel.

STEPHEN MAKES HIS DEFENSE FROM ISRAEL'S HISTORY *
1. THE TIME OF ABRAHAM

7
1   Then the High Priest said,

    "Is this statement true?"

    And Stephen answered,

* For an expanded version of this address, see Appendix, pages 87–93.

"My brothers and my fathers, listen to me. Our glorious God appeared to our forefather Abraham while he was in Mesopotamia before he ever came to live in Haran, and said to him, '*Get thee out of thy land and from thy kindred, and come into a land which I shall shew thee.*' That was how he came to leave the land of the Chaldeans and settle in Haran. And it was from there after his father's death that God moved him into this very land where you are living today. Yet God gave him no part of it as an inheritance, not a foot that he could call his own, and yet promised that it should eventually belong to him and his descendants—even though at the time he had no descendant at all. And this is the way in which God spoke to him: He told him that his descendants should live as strangers in a foreign land where they would become slaves and be ill treated for four hundred years, '*And the nation to which they shall be in bondage will I judge, said God; and after that shall they come forth, and serve me in this place.*'

"Further, He gave him the Agreement of circumcision, so that when Abraham became the father of Isaac he circumcised him on the eighth day.

STEPHEN'S DEFENSE
2. THE PATRIARCHS

"Isaac became the father of Jacob, and Jacob the father of the twelve Patriarchs. Then the Patriarchs in their jealousy of Joseph sold him as a slave into Egypt. But God was with him and saved him from all his troubles and gave him favor and wisdom in the eyes of Pharaoh the King of Egypt. Pharaoh made him Governor of Egypt and put him in charge of his own entire household.

7
8*b*

"Then came the famine over all the land of Egypt and Canaan which caused great suffering, and our forefathers could find no food. But when Jacob heard that there was corn in Egypt he sent our forefathers out of their own country for the first time. It was on their second visit that Joseph was recognized by his brothers, and his ancestry became plain to Pharaoh. Then Joseph sent and invited to come and live with him his father and all his kinsmen, seventy-five people in all. So Jacob came down to Egypt and both he and our fathers ended their days there. After their death they

were carried back into Shechem and laid in the tomb which
Abraham had bought with silver from the sons of Hamor,
Shechem's father.

"But as the time drew near for the fulfillment of the
Promise which God had made to Abraham, our people grew
more and more numerous in Egypt. Finally another king
came to the Egyptian throne who knew nothing of Joseph.
This man cleverly victimized our race. He treated our forefathers abominably, forcing them to expose their infant
children so that the race should die out.

STEPHEN'S DEFENSE
3. GOD'S PROVIDENCE AND MOSES

7   "It was at this very time that Moses was born. He was a
20 child of remarkable beauty, and for three months he was
brought up in his father's house, and then when the time
came for him to be abandoned Pharaoh's daughter adopted
him and brought him up as her own son. So Moses was trained
in all the wisdom of the Egyptians, and became not only an
excellent speaker but a man of action as well.

MOSES' FIRST ABORTIVE ATTEMPT AT RESCUE

7   "Now when he was turned forty the thought came into his
23 mind that he should go and visit his own brothers, the sons of
Israel. He saw one of them being unjustly treated, went to
the rescue and paid rough justice for the man who had been
ill treated by striking down the Egyptian. He fully imagined
that his brothers would understand that God was using him to
rescue them. But they did not understand. Indeed, on the
very next day he came upon two of them who were quarreling and urged them to make peace, saying, 'Men, you are
brothers. What good can come from your injuring each
other?' But the man who was in the wrong pushed his
neighbor away from him, saying to Moses, 'Who made you
a ruler and judge over us? Do you want to kill me as you
killed that Egyptian yesterday?' At that remark Moses fled
and lived as an exile in the land of Midian, where he became
the father of two sons.

MOSES HEARS THE VOICE OF GOD

"It was forty years later in the desert of Mount Sinai   7
that an angel appeared to him in the flames of a burning   30
bush, and the sight filled Moses with wonder. As he approached to look at it more closely the Voice of the Lord
spoke to him, saying, 'I am the God of thy fathers, the God
of Abraham, and the God of Isaac, and the God of Jacob.'
Then Moses trembled and was afraid to look any more. But
the Lord spoke to him and said, '*Loose the shoes from thy
feet: for the place whereon thou standest is holy ground. I
have surely seen the affliction of my people which is in Egypt,
and have heard their groaning, and I am come down to deliver them: and now come, I will send thee into Egypt.*'

BUT ISRAEL REJECTS MOSES

"So this same Moses whom they had rejected in the words,   7
'Who appointed you a ruler and judge?' God sent to be   35
both ruler and deliverer with the help of the angel who
had appeared to him in the bush. This is the man who showed
wonders and signs in Egypt and in the Red Sea, the man who
led them out of Egypt and was their leader in the desert for
forty years. He was Moses, the man who said to the sons of
Israel, '*A prophet shall God raise up unto you from among
your brethren, like unto me.*' In that Church in the desert this
was the man who was the mediator between the angel who
used to talk with him on Mount Sinai and our fathers. This
was the man who received words, living words, which were
to be given to you; and this was the man to whom our forefathers turned a deaf ear! They disregarded him, and in their
hearts hankered after Egypt. They said to Aaron, 'Make us
gods to go before us. For as for this Moses who led us out
of Egypt, we do not know what has become of him.' In
those days they even made a calf, and offered sacrifices to
their idol. They rejoiced in the work of their own hands. So
God turned away from them and left them to worship the
Host of Heaven, as it is written in the book of the
prophets,

Did ye offer unto me slain beasts and sacrifices
Forty years in the wilderness, O house of Israel?

And ye took up the tabernacle of Moloch,
And the star of the god Rephan,
The figures which ye made to worship them:
And I will carry you away beyond Babylon.

GOD'S PRIVILEGES TO ISRAEL

7   "There in the desert our forefathers possessed the Taber-
44 nacle of Witness made according to the pattern which
Moses saw when God instructed him to build it. This Tabernacle was handed down to our forefathers, and they brought
it here when the Gentiles were defeated under Joshua, for
God drove them out as our ancestors advanced. Here it
stayed until the time of David. David won the approval of
God and prayed that he might find a habitation for the God
of Jacob, even though it was not he but Solomon who actually built a house for Him. Yet of course the Most High
does not live in man-made houses. As the prophet says,

The heaven is my throne,
And the earth the footstool of my feet:
What manner of house will ye build me? saith the Lord:
Or what is the place of my rest?
Did not my hand make all these things?

YET ISRAEL IS BLIND AND DISOBEDIENT

7   "You obstinate people, heathen in your thinking, heathen
51 in the way you are listening to me now! It is always the
same—you never fail to resist the Holy Spirit! Just as your
fathers did, so are you doing now. Can you name a single
prophet whom your fathers did not persecute? They killed
the men who long ago foretold the coming of the Just One,
and now in our own day you have become His betrayers
and His murderers. You are the men who have received the
Law of God miraculously, by the hand of angels, *and you
are the men who have disobeyed it*!"

THE TRUTH AROUSES MURDEROUS FURY

7   These words stung them to fury and they ground their
54 teeth at him in rage. Stephen, filled through all his being with
the Holy Spirit, looked steadily up into Heaven. He saw the
glory of God, and Jesus Himself standing at His right hand.

"Look!" he exclaimed, "the heavens are opened and I can see the Son of Man standing at God's right hand!"

At this they put their fingers in their ears. Yelling with fury, as one man they made a rush at him and hustled him out of the city and stoned him. The witnesses * of the execution flung their clothes at the feet of a young man by the name of Saul.

So they stoned Stephen while he called upon God, and said,

"Jesus, Lord, receive my spirit!"

Then, on his knees, he cried in ringing tones,

"Lord, forgive them for this sin."

And with these words he fell into the sleep of death, while Saul gave silent assent to his execution.

WIDESPREAD PERSECUTION FOLLOWS STEPHEN'S DEATH

On that very day a great storm of persecution burst upon the Church in Jerusalem. All Church members except the Apostles were scattered over the countryside of Judaea and Samaria. While reverent men buried Stephen and mourned deeply over him, Saul harassed the Church bitterly. He would go from house to house, drag out both men and women and have them committed to prison. Those who were dispersed by this action went throughout the country, preaching the Good News of the Message as they went. Philip, for instance, went down to the city of Samaria and preached Christ to the people there. His words met with a ready and sympathetic response from the large crowds who listened to him and saw the miracles which he performed. With loud cries evil spirits came out of those who had been possessed by them; and many paralyzed and lame people were cured. As a result there was great rejoicing in that city. 8 1b

A MAGICIAN BELIEVES IN CHRIST

But there was a man named Simon in the city who had been practicing magic for some time and mystifying the people of Samaria. He pretended that he was somebody great and everyone from the lowest to the highest was fascinated by him. Indeed, they used to say, "This man must be that 8 9

---

* In Jewish Law the "witnesses" were also the executioners.

Great Power of God." He had influenced them for a long time, astounding them by his magical practices. But when they had come to believe Philip as he proclaimed to them the Good News of the Kingdom of God and of the Name of Jesus Christ, men and women alike were baptized. Even Simon himself became a believer and after his baptism attached himself closely to Philip. As he saw the signs and remarkable demonstrations of power which took place, he lived in a state of constant wonder.

GOD CONFIRMS SAMARIA'S ACCEPTANCE OF THE GOSPEL

8
14   When the Apostles in Jerusalem heard that Samaria had accepted the Word of God, they sent Peter and John down to them. When these two had arrived they prayed for the Samaritans that they might receive the Holy Spirit for as yet it had not fallen upon any of them. They were living simply as men and women who had been baptized in the Name of the Lord Jesus. So then and there they laid their hands on them and they received the Holy Spirit.

SIMON'S MONSTROUS SUGGESTION IS STERNLY REBUKED

8
18   When Simon saw how the Spirit was given through the Apostles' laying their hands upon people he offered them money with the words,

"Give me this power too, so that if I were to put my hands on anyone he could receive the Holy Spirit."

But Peter said to him,

"To hell with you and your money! * How dare you think you could buy the gift of God? You can have no share or place in this ministry, for your heart is not honest before God. All you can do now is to repent of this wickedness of yours and pray earnestly to God that the evil intention of your heart may be forgiven. For I can see inside you, and I see a man bitter with jealousy and bound with his own sin!"

To this Simon answered,

"Please pray to the Lord for me that none of these things that you have spoken about may come upon me!"

When Peter and John had given their clear witness and spoken the Word of the Lord, they set out for Jerusalem,

* These words are exactly what the Greek means. It is a pity that their real meaning is obscured by modern slang usage.

preaching the Good News to many Samaritan villages as they
went.

PHILIP IS GIVEN A UNIQUE OPPORTUNITY

But an angel of the Lord said to Philip,   8

"Get up and go south down the road which runs from   26
Jerusalem to Gaza, out in the desert."

Philip arose and began his journey. At this very moment an
Ethiopian eunuch, a minister and in fact the treasurer to
Candace, Queen of the Ethiopians, was on his way home after
coming to Jerusalem to worship. He was sitting in his carriage reading the prophet Isaiah. The Spirit said to Philip,

"Approach this carriage, and keep close to it."

Then as Philip ran forward he heard the man reading the
prophet Isaiah, and he said,

"Do you understand what you are reading?"

And he replied,

"How can I unless I have someone to guide me?"

And he invited Philip to get up and sit by his side. The
passage of Scripture he was reading was this:

He was led as a sheep to the slaughter;
And as a lamb before his shearer is dumb,
So he openeth not his mouth:
In his humiliation his judgment was taken away:
His generation who shall declare?
For his life is taken from the earth.

The eunuch turned to Philip and said,

"Tell me, I beg you, about whom is the prophet saying
this—is he speaking about himself or about someone else?"

Then Philip began, and using this Scripture as a starting
point, he told the eunuch the Good News about Jesus. As
they proceeded along the road they came to some water, and
the eunuch said,

"Look, here is some water; is there any reason why I
should not be baptized now?"

And he gave orders for the carriage to stop. Then both of
them got down out of the carriage and Philip baptized the
eunuch. When they came up out of the water the Spirit of
the Lord took Philip away suddenly and the eunuch saw
no more of him, but proceeded on his journey with a heart

full of joy. Philip found himself at Azotus and as he passed
through the countryside he went on telling the Good News
in all the cities until he came to Caesarea.

THE CRISIS FOR SAUL

9
1   But Saul, still breathing murderous threats against the disciples of the Lord, went to the High Priest and begged him
for letters to the synagogues in Damascus, so that if he should
find there any followers of the Way, whether men or women,
he could bring them back to Jerusalem as prisoners.

But on his journey, as he neared Damascus, a light from
Heaven suddenly blazed around him, and he fell to the
ground. Then he heard a Voice speaking to him,

"Saul, Saul, why are you persecuting Me?"

"Who are you, Lord?" he asked.

"I am Jesus Whom you are persecuting," was the reply.
"But now stand up and go into the city and there you will be
told what you must do."

His companions on the journey stood there speechless, for
they had heard the Voice but could see no one. Saul got up
from the ground, but when he opened his eyes he could see
nothing. So they took him by the hand and led him into
Damascus. There he remained sightless for three days, and
during that time he had nothing either to eat or to drink.

GOD'S PREPARATION FOR THE CONVERTED SAUL

9
10   Now in Damascus there was a disciple by the name of
Ananias. The Lord spoke to this man in a dream, calling him
by his name.

"I am here, Lord," he replied.

Then the Lord said to him,

"Get up and go down to the street called Straight and
enquire at the house of Judas for a man named Saul from
Tarsus. At this moment he is praying and he sees in his
mind's eye a man by the name of Ananias coming into the
house, and placing his hands upon him to restore his sight."

But Ananias replied,

"Lord, I have heard on all hands about this man and how
much harm he has done to your holy people in Jerusalem!
Why even now he holds powers from the Chief Priests to
arrest all who call upon Your Name."

But the Lord said to him,

"Go on your way, for this man is My chosen instrument to bear My Name before the Gentiles and their kings, as well as to the sons of Israel. Indeed, I Myself will show him what he must suffer for the sake of My Name."

Then Ananias set out and went to the house, and there he laid his hands upon Saul, and said,

"Saul, brother, the Lord has sent me—Jesus Who appeared to you on your journey here—so that you may recover your sight and be filled with the Holy Spirit."

Immediately something like scales fell from Saul's eyes, and he could see again. He got to his feet and was baptized. Then he took some food and regained his strength.

SAUL'S CONVERSION ASTOUNDS THE DISCIPLES

Saul stayed with the disciples in Damascus for some time. Without delay he proclaimed Jesus in the synagogues declaring that He is the Son of God. All his hearers were staggered and kept saying,

"Isn't this the man who so bitterly persecuted those who called on the Name in Jerusalem, and came down here with the sole object of taking back all such people as prisoners before the Chief Priests?"

But Saul went on from strength to strength, reducing to confusion the Jews who lived at Damascus by proving beyond doubt that this Man is Christ.

THE LONG REVENGE ON THE "RENEGADE" BEGINS

After some time the Jews made a plot to kill Saul, but news of this came to his ears. Although in their murderous scheme the Jews watched the gates day and night for him, Saul's disciples took him one night and let him down through an opening in the wall by lowering him in a basket.

AT JERUSALEM SAUL IS SUSPECT: BARNABAS CONCILIATES

When Saul reached Jerusalem he tried to join the disciples. But they were all afraid of him, finding it impossible to believe that he was a disciple. Barnabas, however, took him by the hand and introduced him to the Apostles, and explained to them how he had seen the Lord on his journey, and how the Lord had spoken to him. He further explained

how Saul had spoken in Damascus with the utmost boldness
in the Name of Jesus. After that Saul joined with them
in all their activities in Jerusalem, preaching fearlessly in
the Name of the Lord. He used to talk and argue with the
Greek-speaking Jews, but they made several attempts on his
life. When the brothers realized this they took him down to
Caesarea and sent him off to Tarsus.

A TIME OF PEACE

9
31

The whole Church throughout Judaea, Galilee and Samaria
now enjoyed a period of peace. It became established and as
it went forward in reverence for the Lord and in the strength-
ening presence of the Holy Spirit, continued to grow in numbers.

PETER HEALS AT LYDDA,

9
32

Now it happened that Peter, in the course of traveling
about among them all, came down to God's people living at
Lydda. There he found a man called Aeneas who had been
bedridden for eight years through paralysis. Peter said to him,
"Aeneas, Jesus Christ heals you! Get up and make your
bed."
He got to his feet at once. And all those who lived in Lydda
and Sharon saw him and turned to the Lord.

AND AGAIN AT JOPPA

9
36

Then there was a woman in Joppa, a disciple called Tabitha,
whose name in Greek was Dorcas (meaning Gazelle). She
was a woman whose whole life was full of good and kindly
actions, but in those days she became seriously ill and died.
So when they had washed her body they laid her in an upper
room. Now Lydda is quite near Joppa, and when the disciples heard that Peter was in Lydda, they sent two men to
him and begged him,
"Please come to us without delay."
Peter got up and went back with them, and when he
arrived in Joppa they took him to the room upstairs. All the
widows stood around him with tears in their eyes, holding
out for him to see the dresses and cloaks which Dorcas used
to make for them while she was with them. But Peter put

them all outside the room and knelt down and prayed. Then he turned to the body and said,

"Tabitha, get up!"

She opened her eyes, and as soon as she saw Peter she sat up. He took her by the hand, helped her to her feet, and then called out to the believers and widows and presented her to them alive. This became known throughout the whole of Joppa and many believed in the Lord. Peter himself remained there for some time, staying with a tanner called Simon.

GOD SPEAKS TO A GOOD-LIVING GENTILE

There was a man in Caesarea by the name of Cornelius, 10 a centurion in what was called the Italian Regiment. He was 1 a deeply religious man who reverenced God, as did all his household. He made many charitable gifts to the people and was a real man of prayer. About three o'clock one afternoon he saw perfectly clearly in a dream an angel of God coming into his room, approaching him, and saying,

"Cornelius!"

He stared at the angel in terror, and said,

"What is it, Lord?"

The angel replied,

"Your prayers and your deeds of charity have gone up to Heaven and are remembered before God. Now send men to Joppa for a man called Simon, who is also known as Peter. He is staying as a guest with another Simon, a tanner, whose house is down by the sea."

When the angel who had spoken to him had gone, Cornelius called out for two of his house servants and a devout soldier, who was one of his personal attendants. He told them the whole story and then sent them off to Joppa.

PETER'S STARTLING VISION

Next day, while these men were still on their journey and 10 approaching the city, Peter went up about midday on to 9 the flat roof of the house to pray. He became very hungry and longed for something to eat. But while the meal was being prepared he fell into a trance and saw the heavens open and something like a great sheet descending upon the earth, let down by its four corners. In it were all kinds of animals, reptiles and birds. Then came a voice which said to him,

"Get up, Peter, kill and eat!"

But Peter said,

"Never, Lord! For not once in all my life have I ever eaten anything common or unclean."

Then the voice spoke to him a second time,

"You must not call what God has cleansed common."

This happened three times, and then the thing was gone, taken back into heaven.

THE MEANING OF THE VISION BECOMES APPARENT

10
17
While Peter was still puzzling about the meaning of the vision which he had just seen, the men sent by Cornelius had arrived asking for the house of Simon. They were in fact standing at the very doorway of the house calling out to enquire if Simon, surnamed Peter, were lodging there. Peter was still thinking deeply about the vision when the Spirit said to him,

"Three men are here looking for you. Get up and go downstairs. Go with them without any misgiving, for I Myself have sent them."

So Peter went down to the men and said,

"I am the man you are looking for; what brings you here?"

They replied,

"Cornelius the centurion, a good-living and God-fearing man, whose character can be vouched for by the whole Jewish people, was commanded by a holy angel to send for you to come to his house, and to listen to your message."

Then Peter invited them in and entertained them.

PETER, OBEYING THE SPIRIT, DISOBEYS JEWISH LAW

10
23b
On the next day he got up and set out with them, accompanied by some of the brothers from Joppa, arriving at Caesarea on the day after that. Cornelius was expecting them and had invited together all his relations and intimate friends. As Peter entered the house Cornelius met him by falling on his knees before him and worshiping him. But Peter roused him with the words,

"Stand up, I am a human being too!"

Then Peter went right into the house in deep conversation

with Cornelius and found that a large number of people had assembled. Then he spoke to them,

"You all know that it is forbidden for a man who is a Jew to associate with, or even visit, a man of another nation. But God has shown me plainly that no man must be called 'common' or 'unclean.' That is why I came here when I was sent for without raising any objection. Now I want to know what made you send for me."

Then Cornelius replied,

"Three days ago, about this time, I was observing the afternoon hour of prayer in my house, when suddenly a man in shining clothes stood before me and said, 'Cornelius, your prayer has been heard and your charitable gifts have been remembered before God. Now you must send to Joppa and invite here a man called Simon whose surname is Peter. He is staying in the house of a tanner by the name of Simon, down by the sea.' So I sent to you without delay and you have been most kind in coming. Now we are all here in the presence of God to listen to everything that the Lord has commanded you to say."

PETER'S MOMENTOUS DISCOVERY

Then Peter began to speak,   10

"In solemn truth I can see now that God is no respecter   34
of persons, but that in every nation the man who reverences
Him and does what is right is acceptable to Him! He has sent
His Message to the sons of Israel by giving us the Good
News of peace through Jesus Christ—He is the Lord of us
all. You must know the story of Jesus of Nazareth—why,
it has spread through the whole of Judaea, beginning from
Galilee after the baptism that John proclaimed. You must
have heard how God anointed Him with the power of the
Holy Spirit, of how He went about doing good and healing
all who suffered from the devil's power—because God was
with Him. Now we are eyewitnesses of everything that He
did, both in the Judaean country and in Jerusalem itself, and
yet they murdered Him by hanging Him on a cross. But
on the third day God raised that same Jesus and let Him be
clearly seen, not indeed by the whole people, but by witnesses
whom God had previously chosen. We are those witnesses,
we who ate and drank with Him after He had risen from the

dead! Moreover, we are the men whom He commanded to preach to the people and bear fearless witness to the fact that He is the One appointed by God to be the Judge of both the living and the dead. It is to Him that all the prophets bear witness, that every man who believes in Him may receive forgiveness of sins in His Name."

THE HOLY SPIRIT CONFIRMS PETER'S ACTION

10
44
While Peter was still speaking these words the Holy Spirit fell upon all who were listening to his message. The Jewish believers who had come with Peter were absolutely amazed that the gift of the Holy Spirit was being poured out on Gentiles also; for they heard them speaking in foreign tongues and glorifying God.

Then Peter exclaimed,

"Could anyone refuse water or object to these men being baptized—men who have received the Holy Spirit just as we did ourselves?"

And he gave orders for them to be baptized in the Name of Jesus Christ. Afterwards they asked him to stay with them for some days.

THE CHURCH'S DISQUIET AT PETER'S ACTION

11
1
Now the Apostles and the brothers who were in Judaea heard that the Gentiles also had received God's Message. So when Peter next visited Jerusalem the Circumcision party were full of criticism, pointing out to him that "you actually went in and shared a meal with uncircumcised men!"

PETER'S EXPLANATION

11
4
But Peter began to explain how the situation had actually arisen.

"I was in the city of Joppa praying," he said, "and while completely unconscious of my surroundings I saw a vision— something like a great sheet coming down towards me, let down from heaven by its four corners. It came right down to me and when I looked at it closely I saw animals and wild beasts, reptiles and birds. Then I heard a voice say to me, 'Get up, Peter, kill and eat.' But I said, 'Never, Lord, for nothing common or unclean has ever passed my lips.' But the voice from Heaven spoke a second time and said, 'You must not call what God has cleansed common!' This happened three times, and then the whole thing was drawn up again into heaven. The extraordinary thing is that at that very moment three men arrived at the house where we were staying, sent to me personally from Caesarea. The Spirit told me to go with these men without any misgiving. And these six of our brothers accompanied me and we went into the man's house. He told us how he had seen the angel standing in his house, saying, 'Send to Joppa and bring Simon, surnamed Peter. He will give you a message which will save both you and your whole household.' While I was beginning to tell them this Message the Holy Spirit fell upon them just as on us at the beginning. There came into my mind the words of our Lord when He said, 'John indeed baptized with water, but you will be baptized with the Holy Spirit.' If then God gave to them exactly the same gift as He gave to us when we believed on the Lord Jesus Christ, who was I to think that I could hinder the working of God?"

THE FLEXIBILITY OF THE YOUNG CHURCH

When they heard this they had no further objection to raise.   11
And they praised God, saying,   18
"Then obviously God has given to the Gentiles as well the gift of repentance which leads to Life."

PERSECUTION HAS SPREAD THE GOSPEL

Now those who had been dispersed by the persecution   11
which arose over Stephen traveled as far as Phoenicia, Cyprus 19
and Antioch, giving the Message as they went to Jews only.
However, among their number were natives of Cyprus and Cyrene, and these men, on their arrival at Antioch, proclaimed their message to the Greeks as well, telling them the Good News of the Lord Jesus. The hand of the Lord was with them, and a great number believed and turned to the Lord. News of these things came to the ears of the Church in Jerusalem and they sent Barnabas to Antioch. When he arrived and saw this working of God's grace, he was delighted. He urged them all to be resolute in their faithfulness to the Lord, for he was a good man, full of the Holy Spirit and of faith. So it happened that a considerable number of people decided for the Lord.

BELIEVERS ARE CALLED "CHRISTIANS" FOR THE FIRST TIME

11   Then Barnabas went to Tarsus to find Saul. When he found
25   him he brought him up to Antioch. Then for a whole year
they met together with the Church and taught a large crowd.
It was in Antioch that the disciples were first given the name
of "Christians."

THE YOUNG CHURCH AND FAMINE RELIEF

11   During this period some prophets came down from Jeru-
27   salem to Antioch. One of them by the name of Agabus stood
up and foretold by the Spirit that there was to be a great
famine throughout the world. (This actually happened in
the days of Claudius.) The disciples determined to send re-
lief to the brothers in Judaea, each contributing as he was
able. This they did, sending their contribution to the elders
there personally through Barnabas and Saul.

HEROD KILLS JAMES AND IMPRISONS PETER

12   It was at this time that King Herod laid violent hands on
1   some of the Church members. James, John's brother, he executed with the sword, and when he found this action pleased
the Jews he went on to arrest Peter as well. It was during
the days of Unleavened Bread that he actually made the
arrest. He put Peter in prison with no less than four platoons
of soldiers to guard him, intending to bring him out to the
people after the Passover. So Peter was closely guarded in
the prison, while the Church prayed to God earnestly on his
behalf.

PETER'S MIRACULOUS RESCUE

12   On the very night before Herod intended to bring him out,
6   Peter was asleep between two soldiers, chained with double
chains, while guards maintained a strict watch in the doorway of the prison. Suddenly an angel of the Lord appeared,
and light shone in the cell. He tapped Peter on the side and
woke him up, saying, "Get up quickly." His chains fell away
from his hands and the angel said to him, "Fasten your belt
and put on your sandals." And he did so. Then the angel
continued, "Wrap your cloak round you and follow me."
So Peter followed him out, not knowing whether what the

angel was doing were real—indeed he felt he must be taking part in a vision. So they passed right through the first gate that led out into the city. This opened for them of its own accord, and they went out and had passed along one street when the angel suddenly vanished from Peter's sight. Then Peter came to himself and said aloud, "Now I know for certain that the Lord has sent His angel to rescue me from the power of Herod and from all that the Jewish people are expecting." As the truth broke upon him he went to the house of Mary, the mother of John surnamed Mark, where many were gathered together in prayer. As he knocked at the door a young maid called Rhoda came to answer it, but on recognizing Peter's voice failed to open the door from sheer joy. Instead she ran inside and reported that Peter was standing on the doorstep. At this they said to her,

"You must be mad!"

But she insisted that it was true. Then they said,

"Then it is his angel."

But Peter continued to stand there knocking on the door, and when they opened it and recognized him they were simply amazed. Peter, however, made a gesture to them to stop talking while he explained to them how the Lord had brought him out of prison. Then he said,

"Go and tell James and the other brothers what has happened."

After this he left them and went on to another place.

PETER'S ESCAPE INFURIATES HEROD

But when morning came there was a great commotion among the soldiers as to what could have happened to Peter. When Herod had had a search put out for him without success, he cross-examined the guards and then ordered their execution. Then he left Judaea and went down to Caesarea and stayed there. 12 18

BUT HEROD DIES A TERRIBLE DEATH

Now Herod was very angry with the people of Tyre and Sidon. They approached him in a body and after winning over Blastus the king's chamberlain, they begged him for peace. They were forced to do this because their country's food supply was dependent on the king's dominions. So on 12 20

an appointed day Herod put on his royal robes, took his seat
on the public throne and made a speech to them. At this the
people kept shouting, "This is a god speaking, not a mere
man!" Immediately an angel of the Lord struck him down
because he did not give God the glory. And in fearful internal
agony he died.

THE MESSAGE CONTINUES TO SPREAD

12
24
But the word of the Lord continued to gain ground and
increase its influence. Barnabas and Saul returned from Jerusalem when they had completed their mission there, bringing
with them John whose surname was Mark.

SAUL AND BARNABAS ARE CALLED TO A SPECIAL TASK

13
1
Now there were in the Church at Antioch both prophets
and teachers—Barnabas, for example, Simeon surnamed Niger,
Lucius the Cyrenian, Manaen the foster brother of the Governor Herod, and Saul. While they were worshiping the Lord
and fasting the Holy Spirit spoke to them, saying,

"Set Barnabas and Saul apart for Me for a task to which
I have called them."

At this, after further fasting and prayer, they laid their
hands on them and set them free for this work. So these two,
sent at the Holy Spirit's command, went down to Seleucia
and from there they sailed off to Cyprus.* On their arrival
at Salamis they began to proclaim God's Message in the
Jewish synagogues, having John as their assistant. As they
made their way through the island as far as Paphos they came
across a man named Bar-Jesus, a Jew who was both a false
prophet and a magician. This man was attached to Sergius
Paulus, the proconsul, who was himself a man of intelligence.
He sent for Barnabas and Saul as he was anxious to hear God's
Message. But Elymas the magician (for that is the translation
of his name) opposed them, doing his best to dissuade the
proconsul from accepting the Faith. Then Saul (who is also
called Paul), filled with the Holy Spirit, eyed him closely
and said,

"You son of the devil, you enemy of all true goodness, you
monster of trickery and evil, is it not high time you gave up

* See Map 1, page 77.

trying to pervert the truth of the Lord? Now listen, the Lord Himself will touch you, for some time you will not see the light of the sun—you will be blind!"

Immediately a mist and then an utter blackness came over his eyes, and he went round trying to find someone to lead him by the hand. When the proconsul saw what had happened he believed, for he was shaken to the core at the Lord's teaching.

SAUL (NOW PAUL) COMES TO ANTIOCH IN PISIDIA

Then Paul and his companions set sail from Paphos and 13 went to Perga in Pamphylia. There John left them and turned 13 back to Jerusalem, but they continued their journey through Perga to the Antioch in Pisidia. They went to the synagogue on the sabbath day and took their seats. After the reading of the law and prophets, the leaders of the synagogue sent to them with a message,

"Men and brothers, if you have any message of encouragement for the people, by all means speak."

PAUL SHOWS THE JEWS WHERE THEIR HISTORY LEADS

So Paul stood up, and motioning with his hand, began: 13

"Men of Israel and all of you who fear God, listen to me. 16 The God of this people Israel chose our fathers and prospered the people even while they were exiles in the land of Egypt. Then He lifted up His arm and led them out of that land. Yes, and He bore with them for forty years in the desert. He destroyed seven nations in the land of Canaan before He gave them that land as their inheritance for some four hundred and fifty years. After that He gave them judges until the time of the prophet Samuel. Then when they begged for a king God gave them Saul the son of Kish, a man of the tribe of Benjamin, to be their king for forty years. After He had deposed him He raised David to the throne, a man of whom God Himself bore testimony in the words, *'I have found David the son of Jesse, a man after my own heart, who shall do all my will.'* From the descendants of this man, according to His Promise, God has brought Jesus to Israel to be their Savior. John came before Him to prepare His way preaching the baptism of repentance for all the people of Israel. Indeed, as John reached the end of his time he said these words: 'What do you think I am? I am not He. But know this,

Someone comes after me Whose shoelace I am not fit to un-
tie!'

13   "Men and brothers, sons of the race of Abraham, and all
26   among you who fear God, it is to us that this Message of
salvation has now been sent! For the people of Jerusalem and
their rulers refused to recognize Him and to understand the
voice of the prophets which are read every sabbath day—
even though in condemning Him they fulfill these very prophecies! For though they found no cause for putting Him to
death, they begged Pilate to have Him executed. And when
they had completed everything that was written about Him,
they took Him down from the Cross and laid Him in a tomb.
But God raised Him from the dead. For many days He was
seen by those who had come up from Galilee to Jerusalem
with Him, and these men are now His witnesses to the people.
And as for us we tell you the good news that the Promise
made to our forefathers has come true—that, in raising up
Jesus, God has fulfilled it for us their children. This is endorsed in the second psalm: '*Thou art my Son, this day have
I begotten thee.*' And as for the fact of God's raising Him
from the dead, never to return to corruption, He has spoken
in these words: 'I will give you the sure mercies of David.'
And then going further He says in another psalm: 'Thou shalt
not suffer thine Holy One to see corruption.' For David, remember, after he had served God's Purpose in his own generation fell asleep and was laid with his ancestors. He did in
fact 'see corruption,' but this Man Whom God raised never
saw corruption! It is therefore imperative, men and brothers,
that every one of you should realise that forgiveness of sins
is proclaimed to you through this Man. And through faith
in Him a man is absolved from all those things from which the
law of Moses could never set him free. Take care then that
this saying of the prophets should never apply to you:

Behold, ye despisers, and wonder, and perish;
For I work a work in your days,
A work which ye shall in no wise believe, if
    one declare it unto you."

PAUL SUCCEEDS IN AROUSING DEEP INTEREST—

As they were going out the people kept on asking them to say all this again on the following sabbath. After the meeting of the synagogue broke up, many of the Jews and devout proselytes followed Paul and Barnabas who spoke personally to them and urged them to put their trust in the grace of God. 13 42

—BUT A WEEK LATER HE MEETS BITTER OPPOSITION

On the next sabbath almost the entire population of the city assembled to hear the Message of God, but when the Jews saw the crowds they were filled with jealousy and contradicted what Paul was saying, covering him with abuse. At this Paul and Barnabas did not mince their words but said, "We felt it our duty to speak the Message of God to you first, but since you spurn it and evidently do not think yourselves fit for eternal life, watch us now as we turn to the Gentiles! Indeed the Lord has commanded us to do so in the words: 13 44

I have set thee for a light of the Gentiles,
That thou shouldest be for salvation unto the uttermost
    part of the earth."

When the Gentiles heard this they were delighted and thanked God for His Message. All those who were destined for eternal life believed, and the Word of the Lord spread over the whole country. But the Jews worked on the feelings of religious and respectable women and some of the leading citizens, and succeeded in starting a persecution against Paul and Barnabas, and expelled them from the district. But they on their part simply shook off the dust from their feet in protest and went on to Iconium. And the disciples continued to be full of joy and the Holy Spirit.

JEWISH BEHAVIOR REPEATS ITSELF

Much the same thing happened at Iconium. On their arrival they went to the Jewish synagogue and spoke with such conviction that a very large number of both Jews and Greeks believed. But the unbelieving Jews stirred up the feelings of 14 1 the Gentiles and poisoned their minds against the brothers. So they remained there for a long time and spoke fearlessly for the Lord, Who made it plain that they were proclaiming the Word of His grace, by allowing them to perform signs and miracles. But the great mass of the people of the city were divided in their opinions, some taking the side of the Jews, and some that of the Apostles. But when a hostile movement arose from both Gentiles and Jews in collaboration with the authorities to insult and stone them, they got to know about it, fled to the Lycaonian cities of Lystra and Derbe, and the surrounding countryside—and from there they continued to proclaim the Gospel.

A MIRACLE IN A COMPLETELY PAGAN CITY

14
8   Now at Lystra a man used to sit who had no strength in his feet. He had in fact been lame from birth and had never been able to walk. It happened that he was listening to Paul as he spoke. Paul, looking him straight in the eye and seeing that he had the faith to be made well, said in a loud voice,

"Stand straight up on your feet!"

And he sprang to his feet and walked. When the crowd saw what Paul had done they shouted in the Lycaonian language,

"The gods have come down to us in human form!"

They began to call Barnabas Jupiter, and Paul Mercury, since he was the chief speaker. What is more, the High Priest of Jupiter whose temple was at the gateway of the city, brought garlanded oxen to the gates and wanted to offer sacrifice with the people. But when the Apostles, Barnabas and Paul, heard of their intention they tore their clothes and rushed into the crowd, crying at the top of their voices,

"Men, men, why are you doing these things? We are only human beings with feelings just like yours! We are here to tell you Good News—that you should turn from these meaningless things to the living God! He is the One Who made Heaven and earth, the sea and all that is in them. In generations gone by He allowed all nations to go on in their own ways—not that He left men without evidence of Himself. For He has shown kindnesses to you; He has sent you rain from heaven and fruitful seasons, giving you food and happiness to your hearts' content."

Yet even with these words they only just succeeded in restraining the crowd from making sacrifices to them.

PAUL IS DOGGED BY HIS JEWISH ENEMIES

Then some Jews arrived from Antioch and Iconium and after turning the minds of the people against Paul they stoned him and dragged him out of the city thinking he was dead. But while the disciples were gathered in a circle round him, Paul got up and walked back into the city. And the very next day he went out with Barnabas to Derbe, and when they had preached the Gospel to that city and made many disciples, they turned back to Lystra, Iconium and Antioch. They put fresh heart into the disciples there, urging them to stand firm in the Faith, and reminding them that "it is *through many tribulations that we must enter into the Kingdom of God.*" They appointed elders for them in each Church, and with prayer and fasting commended these men to the Lord in Whom they had believed. Then they crossed Pisidia and arrived in Pamphylia. They proclaimed their message in Perga and then went down to Attalia. From there they sailed back to Antioch (in Syria) where they had first been commended to the grace of God for the task which they had now completed. When they arrived there they called the Church together and reported to them how greatly God had worked with them and how He had opened the door of faith for the Gentiles. And here at Antioch they spent a considerable time with the disciples.

THE OPPOSITION FROM REACTIONARIES

Then some men came down from Judaea and began to teach the brothers that "unless you are circumcised according to the custom of Moses you cannot be saved." Naturally this caused a serious upset among them and much earnest discussion followed with Paul and Barnabas. Finally it was agreed that Paul and Barnabas should go up to Jerusalem with some of their own people to confer with the Apostles and elders about the whole question.

The Church sent them off on their journey and as they went through Phoenicia and Samaria they told the story of the conversion of the Gentiles and all the brothers were overjoyed to hear about it. On their arrival at Jerusalem they were

welcomed by the Church, by the Apostles and elders, and
they reported how greatly God had worked with them. But
some members of the Pharisees' party who had become believers stood up and declared that it was absolutely essential
that these men be told that they must be circumcised and
observe the Law of Moses.

PETER DECLARES THAT GOD IS DOING SOMETHING NEW

15 The Apostles and elders met to consider this matter. After
6 an exhaustive enquiry Peter stood up and addressed them in
these words:

"Men and brothers, you know that from the earliest days
God chose me as the one from whose lips the Gentiles should
hear the Word and should believe it. Moreover, God Who
knows men's inmost thoughts had plainly shown that this is
so, for when He had cleansed their hearts through their
faith He gave the Holy Spirit to the Gentiles exactly as He
did to us. Why then must you now strain the patience of
God by trying to put on the shoulders of these disciples a
burden which neither our fathers nor we were able to bear?
Surely the fact is that it is by the grace of the Lord Jesus
that we are saved by faith, just as they are!"

These words produced absolute silence, and they listened
to Barnabas and Paul while they gave a detailed account of
the signs and wonders which God had worked through them
among the Gentiles.

JAMES EXPRESSES THE FEELING OF THE MEETING

15 Silence again followed their words and then James made
13 this reply:

"Men and brothers, listen to me. Symeon has shown how
in the first place God chose a people from among the nations
who should bear His Name. This is in full agreement with
what the prophets wrote, as in this Scripture:

After these things I will return,
And I will build again the tabernacle of David, which is
    fallen;
And I will build again the ruins thereof,
And I will set it up:
That the residue of men may seek after the Lord,

And all the Gentiles, upon whom my name is called,
Saith the Lord who maketh these things known from the
    beginning of the world.

"I am firmly of the opinion that we should not put any
additional obstacles before any Gentiles who are turning
towards God. Instead, I think we should write to them telling
them to avoid anything polluted by idols, sexual immorality,
eating the meat of strangled animals, or tasting blood. For
after all, for many generations now Moses has had his
preachers in every city and has been read aloud in the
synagogues every sabbath day."

THE CHURCH'S DEPUTATION: THE MESSAGE TO
GENTILE CHRISTIANS

Then the Apostles, the elders and the whole Church agreed 15
to choose representatives and send them to Antioch with Paul 22
and Barnabas. Their names were Judas, surnamed Barsabas,
and Silas, both leading men of the brotherhood. They carried
with them a letter bearing this message: "The Apostles and
elders who are your brothers send their greetings to the
brothers who are Gentiles in Antioch, Syria and Cilicia.
Since we have heard that some of our number have caused
you deep distress and have unsettled your minds by giving
you a message which certainly did not originate from us, we
are unanimously agreed to send you chosen representatives
with our well loved Barnabas and Paul—men who have risked
their lives for the Name of our Lord Jesus Christ. So we have
sent you Judas and Silas who will give you the same message
personally by word of mouth. For it has seemed right to the
Holy Spirit and to us to lay no further burden upon you
except what is absolutely essential, namely, that you avoid
what has been sacrificed to idols, tasting blood, eating the
meat of what has been strangled, and sexual immorality. Keep
yourselves clear of these things and you will make good
progress. Farewell."

THE MESSAGE IS RECEIVED WITH DELIGHT

So this party, sent off by the Church, went down to 15
Antioch and after gathering the congregation together, 30
handed over the letter to them. And they, when they read it,

were delighted with the encouragement it gave them. Judas and Silas were themselves both inspired preachers and greatly encouraged and strengthened the brothers by many talks to them. Then, after spending some time there, the brothers sent them back in peace to those who had commissioned them. Paul and Barnabas however stayed on in Antioch teaching and preaching the Gospel of the Word of the Lord in company with many others.

PAUL AND BARNABAS FLATLY DISAGREE
BUT THE WORK PROSPERS

15   Some days later Paul spoke to Barnabas,
36   "Now let us go back and visit the brothers in every city where we have proclaimed the Word of the Lord to see how they are." *

Barnabas wanted to take John, surnamed Mark, as their companion. But Paul disapproved of taking with them a man who had deserted them in Pamphylia and was not prepared to go on with them in their work. There was a sharp clash of opinion, so much so that they went their separate ways, Barnabas taking Mark and sailing to Cyprus, while Paul chose Silas and set out on his journey, commended to the grace of the Lord by the brothers as he did so. He traveled through Syria and Cilicia and strengthened the Churches.

PAUL CHOOSES TIMOTHY AS COMPANION

16   He also went to Derbe and Lystra. At Lystra there was a
1   disciple by the name of Timothy whose mother was a Jewish Christian, though his father was a Greek. Timothy was held in high regard by the brothers at Lystra and Iconium, and Paul wanted to take him on as his companion. Everybody knew that his father was a Greek, and Paul therefore had him circumcised because of the attitude of the Jews in these places. As they went on their way through the cities they passed on to them for their observance the decisions which had been reached by the Apostles and elders in Jerusalem. Consequently the Churches grew stronger and stronger in the Faith and their numbers increased daily.

* See Map 2, page 78.

PAUL AND SILAS FIND THEIR JOURNEY DIVINELY DIRECTED

They made their way through Phrygia and Galatia, but the
Holy Spirit prevented them from speaking God's Message in
Asia. When they came to Mysia they tried to enter Bithynia,
but again the Spirit of Jesus would not allow them. So they
passed by Mysia and came down to Troas, where one night
Paul had a vision of a Macedonian man standing and appealing to him in the words: "Come over to Macedonia and help
us!" As soon as Paul had seen this vision we made every effort
to get on to Macedonia, convinced that God had called us to
give them the Good News.

16
6

THE GOSPEL COMES TO EUROPE: A BUSINESSWOMAN
IS CONVERTED

So we set sail from Troas and ran a straight course to
Samothrace, and on the following day to Neapolis. From
there we went to Philippi, a Roman garrison town and the
chief city in that part of Macedonia. We spent some days
in Philippi and on the sabbath day we went out of the city
gate to the riverside, where we supposed there was a place for
prayer. There we sat down and spoke to the women who had
assembled. One of our hearers was a woman named Lydia.
(She came from Thyatira and was a dealer in purple-dyed
cloth.) She was already a believer in God, and He opened her
heart to accept Paul's words. When she and her household had
been baptized she appealed to us, saying,

16
11

"If you are satisfied that I am a true believer in the Lord,
then come down to my house and stay there."

And she insisted on our doing so.

CONFLICT WITH EVIL SPIRITS AND EVIL MEN

One day while we were going to the place of prayer we
were met by a young girl who had a spirit of clairvoyance
and brought her owners a good deal of profit by foretelling
the future. She would follow Paul and the rest of us, crying
out, "These men are servants of the Most High God, and they
are telling you the Way of Salvation." She continued this
behavior for many days, and then Paul, in a burst of irritation,
turned round and spoke to the spirit in her,

16
16

"I command you in the Name of Jesus Christ to come out of her!"

And it came out immediately. But when the girl's owners saw that their hope of making money out of her had disappeared, they seized Paul and Silas and dragged them before the authorities in the market square. There they brought them before the chief magistrates and said,

"These men are Jews and are causing a great disturbance in our city. They are proclaiming customs which it is illegal for us as Roman citizens to accept or practice."

At this the crowd joined in the attack, and the magistrates had them stripped and ordered them to be beaten with rods. Then, after giving them a severe beating, they threw them into prison, instructing the jailer to keep them safe. On receiving such strict orders, he hustled them into the inner jail and fastened their feet securely in the stocks.

THE MIDNIGHT DELIVERANCE: THE JAILER BECOMES A CHRISTIAN

16
25
But about midnight Paul and Silas were praying and singing hymns to God while the other prisoners were listening to them. Suddenly there was a great earthquake, big enough to shake the foundations of the prison. Immediately all the doors flew open and everyone's chains were unfastened. When the jailer woke and saw that the doors of the prison had been opened he drew his sword and was on the point of killing himself, for he imagined that all the prisoners had escaped. But Paul called out to him at the top of his voice,

"Don't hurt yourself—we are all here!"

Then the jailer called for lights, rushed in, and trembling all over, fell at the feet of Paul and Silas. He led them outside, and said,

"Sirs, what must I do to be saved?"

And they replied,

"Believe in the Lord Jesus and then you will be saved, you and your household."

Then they told him and all the members of his household the Message of God. There and then in the middle of the night he took them aside and washed their wounds, and he himself and all his family were baptized without delay. Then he took them into his house and offered them food, he and his whole household overjoyed at finding faith in God.

PAUL, IN A STRONG POSITION, MAKES THE
AUTHORITIES APOLOGIZE

When morning came, the magistrates sent their constables 16
with the message, "Let those men go." The jailer reported 35
this message to Paul, saying,

"The magistrates have sent to have you released. So now
you can leave this place and go on your way in peace."

But Paul said to the constables,

"They beat us publicly without any kind of trial; they
threw us into prison despite the fact that we are Roman
citizens. And now do they want to get rid of us in this
underhand way? Oh no, let them come and take us out themselves!"

The constables reported this to the magistrates, who were
thoroughly alarmed when they heard that they were Romans.
So they came in person and apologized to them, and after
taking them outside the prison, requested them to leave the
city. But on leaving the prison Paul and Silas went to Lydia's
house, and when they had seen the brothers and given them
fresh courage, they took their leave.

BITTER OPPOSITION AT THESSALONICA—

Next they journeyed through Amphipolis and Apollonia 17
and arrived at Thessalonica. Here there was a synagogue of 1
the Jews which Paul entered, following his usual custom. On
three sabbath days he argued with them from the Scriptures,
explaining and quoting passages to prove the necessity for
the death of Christ and His rising again from the dead. "This
Jesus Whom I am proclaiming to you," he concluded, "is
God's Christ!" Some of them were convinced and threw in
their lot with Paul and Silas, and they were joined by a great
many believing Greeks and a considerable number of in-
fluential women. But the Jews, in a fury of jealousy, got hold
of some of the unprincipled loungers of the market place,
gathered a crowd together and set the city in an uproar. Then
they attacked Jason's house in an attempt to bring Paul and
Silas out before the people. When they could not find them
they hustled Jason and some of the brothers before the civic
authorities, shouting, "These are the men who have turned
the world upside down and have now come here, and Jason

has taken them into his house. What is more, all these men act against the decrees of Caesar, saying that there is another King called Jesus!" By these words the Jews succeeded in alarming both the people and the authorities, and they only released Jason and the others after binding them over to keep the peace.

—FOLLOWED BY ENCOURAGEMENT AT BEROEA

17
10
Without delay the brothers despatched Paul and Silas off to Beroea that night. On their arrival there they went to the Jewish synagogue. The Jews proved more generous-minded than those in Thessalonica, for they accepted the Message most eagerly and studied the Scriptures every day to see if what they were now being told were true. Many of them became believers, as did a number of Greek women of social standing and quite a number of men. But when the Jews at Thessalonica found out that God's Message had been proclaimed by Paul at Beroea as well, they came there too to cause trouble and spread alarm among the people. The brothers at Beroea then sent Paul off at once to make his way to the sea coast, but Silas and Timothy remained there. The men who accompanied Paul took him as far as Athens and returned with instructions for Silas and Timothy to rejoin Paul as soon as possible.

PAUL IS IRRITATED BY THE IDOLS OF ATHENS

17
16
Paul had some days to wait at Athens for Silas and Timothy to arrive, and while he was there his soul was exasperated beyond endurance at the sight of a city so completely idolatrous. He felt compelled to discuss the matter with the Jews in the synagogue as well as with God-fearing Gentiles, and he even argued daily in the open market place with the passers-by. While he was speaking there some Epicurean and Stoic philosophers came across him, and some of them remarked,

"What is this cock sparrow trying to say?"

Others said,

"He seems to be trying to proclaim some more gods to us, and outlandish ones at that!"

For Paul was actually proclaiming "Jesus" and "the Resurrection." So they got hold of him and conducted him

to their Council, the Areopagus. There they asked him,
"May we know what this new teaching of yours really is?
You talk of matters which sound strange to our ears, and we
should like to know what they mean." (For all the Athenians,
and even foreign visitors to Athens, had an obsession for any
novelty and would spend their whole time talking about or
listening to anything new.)

PAUL'S SPEECH TO THE "GENTLEMEN OF ATHENS"

So Paul got to his feet in the middle of their Council, and
began,*

"Gentlemen of Athens, my own eyes tell me that you are
in all respects an extremely religious people. For as I made my
way here and looked at your shrines I particularly noticed
one altar on which were inscribed the words, TO GOD THE
UNKNOWN. It is this God Whom you are worshiping in
ignorance that I am here to proclaim to you! God Who made
the world and all that is in it, being Lord of both Heaven
and Earth, does not live in temples made by human hands,
nor is He ministered to by human hands, as though He had
need of anything—seeing that He is the One Who gives to
all men life and breath and everything else. From one forefather He has created every race of men to live over the face
of the whole Earth. He has determined the times of their existence and the limits of their habitation, so that they might
search for God, in the hope that they might feel for Him
and find Him—yes, even though He is not far from any one
of us. Indeed, it is in Him that we live and move and have our
being. Some of your own poets have endorsed this in the
words, 'For we are indeed His children.' If then we are the
children of God, we ought not to imagine God in terms of
gold or silver or stone, contrived by human art or imagination. Now while it is true that God has overlooked the days
of ignorance He now commands all men everywhere to repent. For He has fixed a day on which He will judge the
whole world in justice by the standard of a Man Whom He
has appointed. That this is so He has guaranteed to all men
by raising this Man from the dead."

But when his audience heard Paul talk about a Man being

17

22

---

* For an expanded version of this address, see Appendix, pages 93–96.

raised from the dead some of them laughed outright, but others said,

"We should like to hear you speak again on this subject."

So with this mixed reception Paul retired from their assembly. Yet some did in fact join him and accept the Faith, including Dionysius a member of the Areopagus, a woman by the name of Damaris, and some others as well.

AT CORINTH PAUL IS YET AGAIN REJECTED BY THE JEWS

18
1 Before long Paul left Athens and went on to Corinth where he found a Jew called Aquila, a native of Pontus. This man had recently come from Italy with his wife Priscilla, because Claudius had issued a decree that all Jews should leave Rome. He went to see them in their house and because they practiced the same trade as himself he stayed with them. They all worked together, for their trade was tent-making. Every sabbath Paul used to speak in the synagogue trying to persuade both Jews and Greeks. By the time Silas and Timothy arrived from Macedonia Paul was completely absorbed in preaching the Message, showing the Jews as clearly as he could that Jesus is Christ. However, when they turned against him and abused him he shook his garments at them, and said,

"Your blood be on your own heads! From now on I go with a perfectly clear conscience to the Gentiles."

Then he left them and went to the house of a man called Titius Justus, a man who reverenced God and whose house was next door to the synagogue. Crispus, the leader of the synagogue, became a believer in the Lord, with all his household, and many of the Corinthians who heard the Message believed and were baptized. Then one night the Lord spoke to Paul in a vision,

"Do not be afraid, but go on speaking and let no one silence you, for I Myself am with you and no man shall lift a finger to harm you. There are many in this city who belong to Me."

So Paul settled down there for eighteen months and taught them God's Message.

PAUL'S ENEMIES FAIL TO IMPRESS THE GOVERNOR

18
12 Then, while Gallio was Governor of Achaia, the Jews banded together to attack Paul, and took him to court, saying,

"This man is perverting men's minds to make them worship God in a way that is contrary to the Law."

Paul was all ready to speak, but before he could utter a word Gallio said to the Jews,

"Listen, Jews! If this were a matter of some crime or wrongdoing I might reasonably be expected to put up with you. But since it is a question which concerns a word and names and your own Law, you must attend to it yourselves. I flatly refuse to be judge in these matters."

And he had them ejected from the court. Then they got hold of Sosthenes, the synagogue leader, and beat him in front of the courthouse. But Gallio remained completely unmoved.

PAUL RETURNS, AND REPORTS TO JERUSALEM AND ANTIOCH

Paul stayed for some time after this incident and then took leave of the brothers and sailed for Syria, taking Priscilla and Aquila with him. At Cenchrea he had his hair cut short, for he had taken a solemn vow. They all arrived at Ephesus and there Paul left Aquila and Priscilla, but he himself went into the synagogue and debated with the Jews. When they asked him to stay longer he refused, bidding them farewell with the words, "If it is God's Will I will come back to you again." Then he set sail from Ephesus and went down to Caesarea. Here he disembarked and after paying his respects to the Church in Jerusalem, he went down to Antioch. He spent some time there before he left and proceeded to visit systematically throughout Galatia and Phrygia, putting new heart into all the disciples as he went.

APOLLOS SPEAKS POWERFULLY AT EPHESUS AND CORINTH

Now a Jew called Apollos, a native of Alexandria and a gifted speaker, well versed in the Scriptures, arrived at Ephesus. He had been instructed in the Way of the Lord, and he spoke with burning zeal, teaching the facts about Jesus faithfully even though he knew only the baptism of John. This man began to speak with great boldness in the synagogue. But when Priscilla and Aquila heard him they took him aside and explained the Way of God to him more accurately. Then as he wanted to cross into Achaia, the brothers gave him every encouragement and wrote a letter to the disciples there, asking them to make him welcome. On his arrival he proved a source of great strength to those who had believed through grace, for by his powerful arguments he publicly refuted the Jews, quoting from the Scriptures to prove that Jesus is Christ.

EPHESUS HAS ITS OWN PENTECOST

19
1
While Apollos was in Corinth Paul journeyed through the upper parts of the country and arrived at Ephesus.* There he discovered some disciples, and he asked them,

"Did you receive the Holy Spirit when you believed?"

"No," they replied, "we have never even heard that there is a Holy Spirit."

"Well then, how were you baptized?" asked Paul.

"We were baptized with John's baptism," they replied.

"John's baptism was a baptism to show a change of heart," Paul explained, "but he always told the people that they must believe in the One Who should come after him, that is, in Jesus."

When these men heard this they were baptized in the Name of the Lord Jesus, and then, when Paul had laid his hands on them, the Holy Spirit came upon them and they began to speak with tongues and the inspiration of prophets. (There were about twelve of them in all.)

PAUL'S TWO-YEAR MINISTRY AT EPHESUS

19
8
Then Paul made his way into the synagogue there and for three months he spoke with the utmost confidence, using both argument and persuasion as he talked of the Kingdom of God. But when some of them hardened in their attitude towards the Message and refused to believe it and, what is more, spoke offensively about the Way in public, Paul left them, and withdrew his disciples, and held daily discussions in the lecture hall of Tyrannus. He continued this practice for two years, so that all who lived in Asia, both Greeks and Jews, could hear the Lord's Message. God gave most unusual demonstrations of power through Paul's hands, so much so that people took to the sick any handkerchiefs or clothing which had been in contact with his body, and they were cured of their diseases and their evil spirits left them.

* See Map 3, page 79.

THE VIOLENCE OF EVIL AND THE POWER OF "THE NAME"

But there were some itinerant Jewish exorcists who at- 19
tempted to invoke the Name of the Lord Jesus when dealing 13
with those who had evil spirits. They would say, "I command you in the Name of Jesus Whom Paul preaches." Seven
brothers, sons of a Chief Priest called Sceva, were engaged
in this practice on one occasion, when the evil spirit answered, "Jesus I know, and I am acquainted with Paul, but
who on earth are you?" And the man in whom the evil spirit
was living sprang at them and overpowered them all with
such violence that they rushed out of that house wounded,
with their clothes torn off their backs. This incident became
known to all the Jews and Greeks who were living in
Ephesus, and a great sense of awe came over them all, while
the Name of the Lord Jesus became highly respected. Many
of those who had professed their faith began openly to admit
their former practices. A number of those who had previously
practiced magic collected their books and burned them publicly. (They estimated the value of these books and found it
to be no less than ten thousand dollars.) In this way the Word
of the Lord continued to grow irresistibly in power and influence.

PAUL SPEAKS OF HIS PLANS

After these events Paul set his heart on going to Jerusalem 19
by way of Macedonia and Achaia, remarking,   21
"After I have been there I must see Rome as well."
Then he despatched to Macedonia two of his assistants,
Timothy and Erastus, while he himself stayed for a while
in Asia.

THE SILVERSMITHS' RIOT AT EPHESUS

Now it happened about this time that a great commotion 19
arose concerning the Way. A man by the name of Demetrius, 23
a silversmith who made silver shrines for Diana, provided considerable business for his craftsmen. He gathered these men
together with workers in similar trades, and spoke to them,
"Men," he said, "you all realize how our prosperity depends
on this particular work. If you use your eyes and ears you also

know that not only in Ephesus but practically throughout
Asia this man Paul has succeeded in changing the minds of a
great number of people by telling them that gods made by
human hands are not gods at all. Now the danger is not only
that this trade of ours might fall into disrepute, but also that
the temple of the great goddess Diana herself might come to
be lightly regarded. There is a further danger, that her actual
majesty might be degraded, she whom the whole of Asia, and
indeed the whole world, worships!"

When they heard this they were furiously angry, and
shouted,

"Great is Diana of the Ephesians!"

Soon the whole city was in an uproar, and on a common
impulse the people rushed into the theater dragging with them
Gaius and Aristarchus, two Macedonians who were Paul's
traveling companions. Paul himself wanted to go in among
the crowd, but the disciples would not allow him. Moreover, some high-ranking officials who were Paul's friends sent
to him begging him not to risk himself in the theater. Meanwhile some were shouting one thing and some another, and
the whole assembly was at sixes and sevens, for most of them
had no idea why they had come together at all. A man called
Alexander whom the Jews put forward was pushed into the
forefront of the crowd, and there, after making a gesture
with his hand, he tried to make a speech of defense to the
people. But as soon as they realised that he was a Jew they
shouted as one man for about two hours, "Great is Diana
of the Ephesians!"

PUBLIC AUTHORITY INTERVENES

19   But when the town clerk had finally quietened the crowd,
35   he said,

"Gentlemen of Ephesus, who in the world could be ignorant of the fact that our city of Ephesus is temple guardian
of the great Diana and of the image which fell down from
Jupiter himself? These are undeniable facts and it is your
plain duty to remain calm and do nothing which you might
afterwards regret. For you have brought these men forward, though they are neither plunderers of the temple, nor
have they uttered any blasphemy against our goddess. If
Demetrius and his fellow craftsmen have a charge to bring

against anyone, well, the courts are open and there are magistrates; let them take legal action. But if you require anything beyond that then it must be resolved in the regular Assembly. For all of us are in danger of being charged with rioting over today's events—particularly as we have no real excuse to offer for this commotion."

And with these words he dismissed the assembly.

PAUL DEPARTS ON HIS SECOND VISIT TO EUROPE

After this disturbance had died down, Paul sent for the disciples and after speaking encouragingly said good-bye to them, and went on his way to Macedonia.* As he made his journey through these districts he spoke many heartening words to the people and then went on to Greece, where he stayed for three months. Then when he was on the point of setting sail for Syria the Jews made a further plot against him and he decided to make his way back through Macedonia. His companions on the journey were Sopater a Beroean, the son of Pyrrhus; two Thessalonians, Aristarchus and Secundus; Gaius from Derbe, Timothy, and two Asians, Tychicus and Trophimus. This party proceeded to Troas to await us there, while we sailed from Philippi after the days of Unleavened Bread, and joined them five days later at Troas, where we spent a week.

PAUL'S ENTHUSIASM LEADS TO AN ACCIDENT

On the first day of the week, when we were assembled for the breaking of bread, Paul, since he intended to leave on the following day, began to speak to them and prolonged his address until almost midnight. There were a great many lamps burning in the upper room where we met, and a young man called Eutychus who was sitting on the window sill fell fast asleep as Paul's address became longer and longer. Finally, completely overcome by sleep, he fell to the ground from the third story and was picked up as dead. But Paul went down, bent over him and holding him gently in his arms, said,

"Don't be alarmed; he is still alive."

Then he went upstairs again and, when he had broken bread and eaten, continued a long earnest talk with them

20
1

20
7

* See Map 3, page 79.

until daybreak, and so finally departed. As for the boy, they took him home alive, feeling immeasurably relieved.

WE SAIL TO MILETUS

20   Meanwhile we had gone aboard the ship and sailed on ahead
13 for Assos, intending to pick up Paul there, for that was the arrangement he had made, since he himself had planned to go overland. When he met us on our arrival at Assos we took him aboard and went on to Mitylene. We sailed from there and arrived off the coast of Chios the next day. On the day following we crossed to Samos, and the day after that we reached Miletus. For Paul had decided to sail past Ephesus with the idea of spending as little time as possible in Asia. He hoped, if it should prove possible, to reach Jerusalem in time for the Day of Pentecost.

PAUL'S MOVING FAREWELL MESSAGE TO THE ELDERS OF EPHESUS

20   At Miletus he sent to Ephesus to summon the elders of the
17 Church. On their arrival he addressed them in these words:
"I am sure you know how I have lived among you ever since I first set foot in Asia. You know how I have served the Lord most humbly and what tears I have shed over the trials that have come to me through the plots of the Jews. You know I have never shrunk from telling you anything that was for your good, nor from teaching you in public or in your own homes. On the contrary I have most emphatically urged upon both Jews and Greeks repentance towards God and faith in our Lord Jesus. And now here I am, compelled by the Spirit to go to Jerusalem. I do not know what may happen to me there, except that the Holy Spirit warns me that imprisonment and persecution await me in every city that I visit. But frankly I do not consider my own life valuable to me so long as I can finish my course and complete the ministry which the Lord Jesus has given me in declaring the Good News of the grace of God. Now I know well enough that not one of you among whom I have moved as I preached the Kingdom of God will ever see my face again. That is why I must tell you solemnly today that my conscience is clear as far as any of you is concerned, for I have never shrunk from declaring to you the complete Will of God. Now be on your guard for yourselves and for every flock of which the Holy

Spirit has made you guardians—you are to be shepherds to the Church of God, which He won at the cost of His own blood. I know that after my departure savage wolves will come in among you without mercy for the flock. Yes, and even from among you men will arise speaking perversions of the truth, trying to draw away the disciples and make them followers of themselves. This is why I tell you to keep on the alert, remembering that for three years I never failed night and day to warn every one of you, even with tears in my eyes. Now I commend you to the Lord and to the Message of His grace which can build you up and give you your place among all those who are consecrated to God. I have never coveted anybody's gold or silver or clothing. You know well enough that these hands of mine have provided for my own needs and for my companions. In everything I have shown you that by such hard work we must help the weak and must remember the words of the Lord Jesus when He said, 'Giving is a happier thing than receiving.'"

With these words he knelt down with them all and prayed. All of them were in tears, and throwing their arms round Paul's neck they kissed him affectionately. What saddened them most of all was his saying that they would never see his face again. And they went with him down to the ship.

THE BROTHERS AT EPHESUS WARN PAUL NOT TO GO TO JERUSALEM

When we had finally said farewell to them we set sail, 21 running a straight course to Cos, and the next day we went 1 to Rhodes and from there to Patara. Here we found a ship bound for Phoenicia, and we went aboard her and set sail. After sighting Cyprus and leaving it on our left we sailed for Syria and put in at Tyre, since that was where the ship was to discharge her cargo. We sought out the disciples there and stayed with them for a week. They felt led by the Spirit again and again to warn Paul not to go up to Jerusalem. But when our time was up we left them and continued our journey. They all came out to see us off, bringing their wives and children with them, accompanying us till we were outside the city. Then kneeling down on the beach we prayed and said good-bye to each other. Then we went aboard the ship, while the disciples went back home. We sailed away from Tyre and arrived at Ptolemais. We greeted the brothers there and stayed with them for just one day. On the following day we left and proceeded to Caesarea and there we went to stay at the house of Philip the evangelist, one of the seven deacons. He had four unmarried daughters, all of whom spoke by the Spirit of God. During our stay there of several days a prophet by the name of Agabus came down from Judaea. When he came to see us he took Paul's girdle and used it to tie his own hands and feet together, saying, "The Holy Spirit says this: The man to whom this girdle belongs will be bound like this by the Jews in Jerusalem and handed over to the Gentiles!"

WE ALL WARN PAUL, BUT HE IS IMMOVABLE

21
12
When we heard him say this, we and the people there begged Paul not to go up to Jerusalem. Then Paul answered us,

"What do you mean by unnerving me with all your tears? I am perfectly prepared not only to be bound but to die in Jerusalem for the sake of the Name of the Lord Jesus."

Since he could not be dissuaded all we could do was to say, "May the Lord's Will be done," and hold our tongues.

PAUL IS WARMLY WELCOMED AT FIRST

21
15
After this we made our preparations and went up to Jerusalem. Some of the disciples from Caesarea accompanied us and they brought us to the house of Mnason, a native of Cyprus and one of the earliest disciples, with whom we were going to stay. On our arrival at Jerusalem the brothers gave us a very warm welcome. On the following day Paul went with us to visit James, and all the elders were present. When he had greeted them he gave them a detailed account of all that God had done among the Gentiles through his ministry, and they, on hearing this account, glorified God. Then they said to him,

"You know, brother, how many thousands there are among the Jews who have become believers, and that every one of these is a staunch upholder of the Law. They have been told about you—that you teach all Jews who live among the Gentiles to disregard the Law of Moses, and tell them not to circumcise their children nor observe the old customs. What will happen now, for they are simply bound to hear

that you have arrived? Now why not follow this suggestion
of ours? We have four men here under a vow. Suppose you
join them and be purified with them, pay their expenses so
that they may have their hair cut short, and then everyone
will know there is no truth in the stories about you, but
that you yourself observe the Law. As for those Gentiles who
have believed, we have sent them a letter with our decision
that they should abstain from what has been offered to idols,
from blood and from what has been strangled, and from
sexual immorality."

BUT HIS ENEMIES ATTEMPT TO MURDER HIM

So Paul joined the four men and on the following day,   21
after being purified with them, went into the Temple to give   26
notice of the time when the period of purification would be
finished and an offering would be made on behalf of each one
of them. The seven days were almost over when the Jews
from Asia caught sight of Paul in the Temple. They stirred
up the whole crowd and seized him, shouting, "Men of Israel,
help! This is the man who is teaching everybody everywhere
to despise our people, our Law and this place. Why, he has
even brought Greeks into the Temple and he has defiled this
holy place!" For they had previously seen Trophimus the
Ephesian with Paul in the city and they had concluded that
Paul had brought him into the Temple. The whole city was
stirred by this speech and a mob collected who seized Paul
and dragged him outside the Temple, and the doors were
slammed behind him.

PAUL IS RESCUED BY ROMAN SOLDIERS

They were trying to kill him when a report reached the   21
ears of the colonel of the regiment that the whole of Jeru-   31
salem was in an uproar. Without a moment's delay he took
soldiers and centurions and ran down to them. When they saw
the colonel and the soldiers they stopped beating Paul. The
colonel came up to Paul and arrested him and ordered him
to be bound with two chains. Then he enquired who the man
was and what he had been doing. Some of the crowd shouted
one thing and some another, and since he could not be certain
of the facts because of the shouting that was going on, the
colonel ordered him to be brought to the barracks. When Paul

got to the steps he was actually carried by the soldiers because of the violence of the mob. For the mass of the people followed, shouting, "Kill him!" Just as they were going to take him into the barracks Paul asked the colonel,

"May I say something to you?"

"So you know Greek, do you?" the colonel replied. "Aren't you that Egyptian who not long ago raised a riot and led those four thousand assassins into the desert?"

"I am a Jew," replied Paul. "I am a man of Tarsus, a citizen of that not insignificant city. I ask you to let me speak to the people."

PAUL ATTEMPTS TO DEFEND HIMSELF

21
40   On being given permission Paul stood on the steps and made a gesture with his hand to the people. There was a deep hush as he began to speak to them in Hebrew.

22
1   "My brothers and my fathers, listen to what I have to say in my own defense."

As soon as they heard him addressing them in Hebrew the silence became intense.

"I myself am a Jew," Paul went on. "I was born in Tarsus in Cilicia, but I was brought up here in this city, I received my training at the feet of Gamaliel, and I was schooled in the strictest observance of our fathers' Law. I was as much on fire with zeal for God as you all are today. I am also the man who persecuted this Way to the death, arresting both men and women and throwing them into prison, as the High Priest and the whole Council can readily testify. Indeed, it was after receiving letters from them to their brothers in Damascus that I was on my way to that city intending to arrest any followers of the Way I could find there and bring them back to Jerusalem for punishment. Then this happened to me. As I was on my journey and getting near to Damascus, about midday a great light from Heaven suddenly blazed around me. I fell to the ground, and I heard a Voice saying to me, 'Saul, Saul, why are you persecuting Me?' I replied, 'Who are you, Lord?' He said to me, 'I am Jesus of Nazareth Whom you are persecuting.' My companions naturally saw the light, but they did not hear the Voice of the One Who was talking to me. 'What am I to do, Lord?' I asked. And the Lord told me,

'Get up and go to Damascus and there you will be told of all that has been determined for you to do.' I was blinded by the brightness of that light and my companions had to take me by the hand as we went on to Damascus. There, there was a man called Ananias, a reverent observer of the Law and a man highly respected by all the Jews who lived there. He came to visit me and as he stood by my side said, 'Saul, brother, you may see again!' At once I regained my sight and looked up at him. 'The God of our fathers,' he went on, 'has chosen you to know His Will, to see the Righteous One, to hear words from His own lips, so that you may become His witness before all men of what you have seen and heard. And now what are you waiting for? Get up and be baptized! Be clean from your sins as you call on His Name.'

PAUL CLAIMS THAT GOD SENT HIM TO THE GENTILES

"Then it happened that after my return to Jerusalem, while I was at prayer in the Temple, unconscious of everything else, I saw Him and He said to me, 'Make haste and leave Jerusalem at once, for they will not accept your testimony about Me.' And I said, 'But, Lord, they know how I have been through all the synagogues imprisoning and beating all those who believe in You. They know also that when the blood of Your martyr Stephen was shed I stood by, giving my approval— why, I was even holding in my arms the outer garments of those who killed him.' But He said to me, 'Go, for I will send you far away to the Gentiles.' " 22 17

THE CONSEQUENCE OF PAUL'S SPEECH

They had listened to him until he said this, but now they raised a great shout, 22 22

"Kill him, and rid the earth of such a man! He is not fit to live!"

As they were yelling and ripping their clothes and hurling dust into the air, the colonel gave orders to bring Paul into the barracks and directed that he should be examined by scourging, so that he might discover the reason for such an uproar against him. But when they had strapped him up, Paul spoke to the centurion standing by,

"Is it legal for you to flog a man who is a Roman citizen, and untried at that?"

On hearing this the centurion went in to the colonel and reported to him, saying,

"Do you realize what you were going to do? This man is a Roman citizen!"

Then the colonel himself came up to Paul and said,

"Tell me, are you a Roman citizen?"

And he said,

"Yes."

Whereupon the colonel replied,

"It cost me a good deal to get my citizenship."

"Ah," replied Paul, "but I was born a citizen."

Then those who had been about to examine him left hurriedly, while even the colonel himself was alarmed at discovering that Paul was a Roman and that he had had him bound.

ROMAN FAIR-MINDEDNESS

22
30 Next day the colonel, determined to get to the bottom of Paul's accusation by the Jews, released him and ordered the assembly of the Chief Priests and the whole Sanhedrin. Then he took Paul down and placed him in front of them.

PAUL AGAIN ATTEMPTS DEFENSE

23
1 Paul looked steadily at the Sanhedrin and spoke to them, "Men and brothers, I have lived my life with a perfectly clear conscience before God up to the present day—" Then Ananias the High Priest ordered those who were standing near to strike him on the mouth. At this Paul said to him,

"God will strike you, you whitewashed wall! How dare you sit there judging me by the Law and give orders for me to be struck, which is clean contrary to the Law?"

Those who stood by said,

"Do you mean to insult God's High Priest?"

But Paul said,

"My brothers, I did not know that he was the High Priest, for it is written:

Thou shalt not speak evil of a ruler of thy people."

PAUL SEIZES HIS OPPORTUNITY

Then Paul, realizing that part of the Council were Sad- 23
ducees and the other part Pharisees, raised his voice and said 6
to them,

"I am a Pharisee, the son of Pharisees. It is for my hope in
the resurrection of the dead that I am on trial!"

At these words an immediate tension arose between the
Pharisees and the Sadducees, and the meeting was divided.
For the Sadducees claim that there is no resurrection and that
there is neither angel nor spirit, while the Pharisees believe
in all three. A great uproar ensued and some of the scribes
of the Pharisees' party jumped to their feet and protested
violently,

"We find nothing wrong with this man! Suppose some
angel or spirit has really spoken to him?"

As the tension mounted the colonel began to fear that Paul
would be torn to pieces between them. He therefore ordered
his soldiers to come down and rescue him from them and
bring him back to the barracks.

GOD'S DIRECT ENCOURAGEMENT TO PAUL

That night the Lord stood by Paul, and said, 23

"Take heart! For as you have witnessed boldly for me in 11
Jerusalem so you must give your witness for me in Rome."

PAUL'S ACUTE DANGER

Early in the morning the Jews made a conspiracy and 23
bound themselves by a solemn oath that they would neither 12
eat nor drink until they had killed Paul. Over forty of them
were involved in this plot, and they approached the Chief
Priests and elders and said,

"We have bound ourselves by a solemn oath to let nothing
pass our lips until we have killed Paul. Now you and the
Council must make it plain to the colonel that you want him
to bring Paul down to you, suggesting that you want to
examine his case more closely. We shall be standing by ready
to kill him before he gets here."

LEAKAGE OF INFORMATION LEADS TO PAUL'S PROTECTION

23   However, Paul's nephew got wind of this plot and he
16   came and found his way into the barracks and told Paul about
it. Paul called one of the centurions and said,

"Take this young man to the colonel for he has something
to report to him."

So the centurion took him and brought him into the
colonel's presence, and said,

"The prisoner Paul called me and requested that this young
man should be brought to you as he has something to say to
you."

The colonel took his hand and drew him aside (where
they could not be overheard), and asked,

"What have you got to tell me?"

And he replied,

"The Jews have agreed to ask you to bring Paul down to
the Sanhedrin tomorrow as though they were going to enquire more carefully into his case. But I beg you not to let
them persuade you. For more than forty of them are waiting for him—they have sworn a solemn oath that they will
neither eat nor drink until they have killed him. They are all
ready at this moment—all they want now is for you to give
the order."

At this the colonel dismissed the young man with the
caution,

"Don't let a soul know that you have given me this information."

Then he summoned two of his centurions, and said,

"Get two hundred men ready to proceed to Caesarea,
with seventy horsemen and two hundred spearmen, by nine
o'clock tonight." (Mounts were also to be provided to carry
Paul safely to Felix the Governor.)

THE ROMAN VIEW OF PAUL'S POSITION

23   He further wrote a letter to Felix of which this is a copy:
25   "Claudius Lysias sends greeting to His Excellency the Governor Felix,

"This man had been seized by the Jews and was on the
point of being murdered by them when I arrived with my

troops and rescued him, since I had discovered that he was a Roman citizen. Wishing to find out what the accusation was that they were making against him, I had him brought down to their Sanhedrin. There I discovered he was being accused over questions of their law, and that there was no charge against him which deserved either death or imprisonment. Now however, that I have received private information of a plot against his life, I have sent him to you without delay. At the same time I have notified his accusers that they must make their charges against him in your presence."

PAUL IS TAKEN INTO PROTECTIVE CUSTODY

The soldiers, acting on their orders, took Paul and, riding 23 through that night, brought him down to Antipatris. Next 31 day they returned to the barracks, leaving the horsemen to accompany him further. They went into Caesarea and after delivering the letter to the Governor, they handed Paul over to him. When the Governor had read the letter he asked Paul what province he came from, and on learning that he came from Cilicia, he said,

"I will hear your case as soon as your accusers arrive."

Then he ordered him to be kept prisoner in Herod's palace.

THE "PROFESSIONAL" PUTS THE CASE AGAINST PAUL

Five days later Ananias the High Priest came down him- 24 self with some of the elders and a lawyer by the name of 1 Tertullus. They presented their case against Paul before the Governor, and when Paul had been summoned, Tertullus began the prosecution in these words:

"We owe it to you personally, Your Excellency, that we enjoy lasting peace, and we know that it is due to your fore-sight that the nation enjoys improved conditions of living. At all times, and indeed everywhere, we acknowledge these things with the deepest gratitude. However—for I must not detain you too long—I beg you to give us a brief hearing with your customary kindness. The simple fact is that we have found this man a pestilential disturber of the peace among the Jews all over the world. He is a ringleader of the Nazareth sect, and he was on the point of desecrating the Temple when we overcame him. But you yourself will soon discover from the man himself all the facts about which we are accusing him."

PAUL IS GIVEN THE CHANCE TO DEFEND HIMSELF

24
9 While Tertullus was speaking the Jews kept joining in, asserting that these were the facts. Then Paul, at a nod from the Governor, made his reply:

"I am well aware that you have been Governor of this nation for many years, and I can therefore make my defense with every confidence. You can easily verify the fact that it is not more than twelve days ago that I went up to worship at Jerusalem. I was never found either arguing with anyone in the Temple or gathering a crowd, either in the synagogues or in the open air. These men are quite unable to prove the charges they are now making against me. I will freely admit to you, however, that I do worship the God of our fathers according to the Way which they call a heresy, although in fact I believe in the scriptural authority of both the Law and prophets. I have the same hope in God which they themselves hold, that there is to be a resurrection of both good men and bad. With this hope before me I do my utmost to live my whole life with a clear conscience before God and man.

PAUL HAS NOTHING TO HIDE

24
17 "It was in fact after several years' absence from Jerusalem that I came back to make charitable gifts to my own nation and to make my offerings. It was in the middle of these duties that they found me, a man purified in the Temple. There was no mob and there was no disturbance until these Jews from Asia came, who should in my opinion have come before you and made their accusation, if they had anything against me. Or else, let these men themselves speak out now and say what crime they found me guilty of when I stood before the Sanhedrin—unless it was that one sentence that I shouted as I stood among them. All I said was this, 'It is about the resurrection of the dead that I am on trial before you this day.' "

FELIX DEFERS DECISION

24
22 Then Felix, who was better acquainted with the Way than most people, adjourned the case and said,

"As soon as Colonel Lysias arrives I will give you my decision."

Then he gave orders to the centurion to keep Paul in custody, but to grant him reasonable liberty and allow any of his personal friends to look after his needs.

FELIX PLAYS FOR SAFETY—AND HOPES FOR PERSONAL GAIN

Some days later Felix arrived with his wife Drusilla, herself a Jewess, and sent for Paul, and heard what he had to say about faith in Christ Jesus. But while Paul was talking about goodness, self-control and the judgment that is to come, Felix became alarmed, and said,

"You may go for the present. When I find a convenient moment I will send for you again."

At the same time he nursed a secret hope that Paul would pay him money—which is why Paul was frequently summoned to come and talk with him. However, when two full years had passed, Felix was succeeded by Porcius Festus and, as he wanted to remain in favor with the Jews, he left Paul still a prisoner.

FELIX'S SUCCESSOR BEGINS HIS DUTIES WITH VIGOR—

Three days after Festus had taken over his province he went up from Caesarea to Jerusalem. The Chief Priests and elders of the Jews informed him of the case against Paul and begged him as a special favor to have Paul sent to Jerusalem. They themselves had already made a plot to kill him on the way. But Festus replied that Paul was in custody in Caesarea, and that he himself was going there shortly.

"What you must do," he told them, "is to provide some competent men of your own to go down with me and if there is anything wrong with the man they can present their charges against him."

Festus spent not more than eight or ten days among them at Jerusalem and then went down to Caesarea. On the day after his arrival he took his seat on the Bench and ordered Paul to be brought in. As soon as he arrived the Jews from Jerusalem stood up on all sides of him, bringing forward many serious accusations which they were quite unable to substantiate. Paul, in his defense, maintained,

"I have committed no offense in any way against the Jewish Law, or against the Temple or against Caesar."

—BUT IS AFRAID OF ANTAGONIZING THE JEWS

25
9
But Festus, wishing to gain the goodwill of the Jews, spoke direct to Paul,

"Are you prepared to go up to Jerusalem and stand your trial over these matters in my presence there?"

But Paul replied,

"I am standing in Caesar's court and that is where I should be judged. I have done the Jews no harm, as you very well know. It comes to this: if I were a criminal and had committed some crime which deserved the death penalty, I should not try to evade sentence of death. But as in fact there is no truth in the accusations these men have made, I am not prepared to be used as a means of gaining their favor—*I appeal to Caesar!*"

Then Festus, after a conference with his advisers, replied to Paul,

"You have appealed to Caesar—then to Caesar you shall go!"

FESTUS OUTLINES PAUL'S CASE TO AGRIPPA

25
13
Some days later King Agrippa and Bernice arrived at Caesarea on a state visit to Festus. They prolonged their stay for some days, and this gave Festus an opportunity of laying Paul's case before the king.

"I have a man here," he said, "who was left in prison by Felix. When I was in Jerusalem the Chief Priests and Jewish elders made allegations against him and demanded his conviction! I told them that the Romans were not in the habit of giving anybody up to please anyone, until the accused had had the chance of facing his accusers personally and been given the opportunity of defending himself on the charges made against him. Since these Jews came back here with me, I wasted no time but on the very next day I took my seat on the Bench and ordered the man to be brought in. But when his accusers got up to speak they did not charge him with any such crimes as I had anticipated. Their differences with him were about their own religion and concerning a certain Jesus Who had died, but Who Paul claimed was still alive. I did not feel

qualified to investigate such matters and so I asked the man
if he were willing to go to Jerusalem and stand his trial over
these matters there. But when he appealed to have his case
reserved for the decision of His Majesty himself, I ordered
him to be kept in custody until such time as I could send
him to Caesar."

Then Agrippa said to Festus,

"I have been wanting to hear this man myself."

"Then you shall hear him tomorrow," replied Festus.

FESTUS FORMALLY EXPLAINS THE DIFFICULTY OF PAUL'S CASE

When the next day came, Agrippa and Bernice proceeded   25
to the audience chamber with great pomp and ceremony,   23
with an escort of military officers and prominent townsmen.
Festus ordered Paul to be brought in and then he spoke:

"King Agrippa and all of you who are present, you see
here the man about whom the whole Jewish people both at
Jerusalem and in this city have petitioned me. They din it
into my ears that he ought not to live any longer, but I for
my part discovered nothing that he has done which deserves
the death penalty. And since he has appealed to His Majesty,
I have decided to send him to Rome. Frankly, I have nothing
specific to write to the Emperor about him, and I have therefore brought him forward before you all, and especially
before you, King Agrippa, so that from your examination of
him there may emerge some charge which I may put in writing. For it seems ridiculous to me to send a prisoner before the
Emperor without indicating the charges against him."

Then Agrippa said to Paul,

"You have our permission to speak for yourself."

PAUL REPEATS HIS STORY ON A STATE OCCASION

So Paul, with that characteristic gesture of the hand, began   26
his defense: *   1b

"King Agrippa, in answering all the charges that the Jews
have made against me, I must say how fortunate I consider
myself to be in making my defense before you personally today. For I know that you are thoroughly familiar with all the
customs and disputes that exist among the Jews. I therefore
ask you to listen to me patiently.

* For an expanded version of this speech, see Appendix, pages 97–103.

"The fact that I lived from my youth upwards among my own people in Jerusalem is well known to all Jews. They have known all the time, and could witness to the fact if they wished, that I lived as a Pharisee according to the strictest sect of our religion. Even today I stand here on trial because of a hope that I hold in a Promise that God made to our forefathers—a Promise for which our twelve tribes serve God zealously day and night, hoping to see it fulfilled. It is about this hope, Your Majesty, that I am being accused by Jews! Why does it seem incredible to you all that God should raise the dead? I once thought it my duty to oppose with the utmost vigor the Name of Jesus of Nazareth. Yes, that is what I did in Jerusalem, and I had many of God's people imprisoned on the authority of the Chief Priests, and when they were on trial for their lives I gave my vote against them. Many and many a time in all the synagogues I had them punished and I used to try and force them to deny their Lord. I was mad with fury against them, and I hounded them to distant cities. Once, Your Majesty, on my way to Damascus on this business, armed with the full authority and commission of the Chief Priests, at midday I saw a light from Heaven, far brighter than the sun, blazing about me and my fellow travelers. We all fell to the ground and I heard a Voice saying to me in Hebrew, 'Saul, Saul, why are you persecuting Me? It is not easy for you to kick against your own conscience.' 'Who are you, Lord?' I said. And the Lord said to me, 'I am Jesus Whom you are persecuting. Now get up and stand on your feet for I have shown Myself to you for a reason—you are chosen to be My servant and a witness of what you have seen of Me today, and of other visions of Myself which I will give you. I will keep you safe both from your own people and from the Gentiles to whom I now send you. I send you to open their eyes, to turn them from darkness to light, from the power of Satan to God Himself, so that they may know forgiveness of their sins and take their place with all those who are made holy by their faith in Me.' After that, King Agrippa, I could not disobey the heavenly vision. But both in Damascus and in Jerusalem, through the whole of Judaea, and to the Gentiles, I preached that men should repent and turn to God and live lives to prove their change of heart. This is why the Jews seized me in the Temple and tried to kill me. To this day I have received help from God Himself, and I stand here as a witness to high and low, adding nothing to what the prophets and Moses foretold should take place, that is, that Christ should suffer, that He should be the first to rise from the dead, and so proclaim the message of light both to our people and to the Gentiles!"

FESTUS CONCLUDES THAT PAUL'S ENTHUSIASM IS INSANITY

While he was thus defending himself Festus burst out, 26 "You are raving, Paul! All your learning has driven 24 you mad!"

But Paul replied,

"I am not mad, Your Excellency. I speak nothing but the sober truth. The king knows of these matters, and I can speak freely before him. I cannot believe that any of these matters has escaped his notice, for it has been no hole-and-corner business. King Agrippa, do you believe the prophets? But I know that you believe them."

"Much more of this, Paul," returned Agrippa, "and you will be making me a Christian!"

"Ah," replied Paul, "whether it means 'much more' or 'only a little,' I would to God that you and all who can hear me this day might stand where I stand—but without these chains!"

THE ROMAN OFFICIALS CONSIDER PAUL INNOCENT

Then the king rose to his feet and so did the Governor and 26 Bernice and those sitting with them, and when they had re- 30 tired from the assembly they discussed the matter among themselves and agreed, "This man has done nothing to deserve either death or imprisonment."

Agrippa remarked to Festus,

"He might easily have been discharged if he had not appealed to Caesar."

THE LAST JOURNEY BEGINS

As soon as it was decided that we should sail away to 27 Italy, Paul and some other prisoners were turned over to a 1 centurion named Julius, of the Emperor's own regiment.

We embarked on a ship hailing from Adramyttium, bound
for the Asian ports, and set sail.* Among our company was
Aristarchus, a Macedonian from Thessalonica. On the following day we put in at Sidon, where Julius treated Paul most
considerately by allowing him to visit his friends and accept
their hospitality. From Sidon we put to sea again and sailed
to leeward of Cyprus, since the wind was against us. Then,
when we had crossed the gulf that lies off the coasts of Cilicia
and Pamphylia, we arrived at Myra in Lycia. There the
centurion found an Alexandrian ship bound for Italy and put
us aboard her. For several days we beat slowly up to wind-
ward and only just succeeded in arriving off Cnidus. Then,
since the wind was still blowing against us, we sailed under the
lee of Crete, and rounded Cape Salmone. Coasting along
with difficulty we came to a place called Fair Havens, near
which is the city of Lasea. We had by now lost a great deal
of time and sailing had already become dangerous as it was
so late in the year.

PAUL'S WARNING IS DISREGARDED

27   So Paul warned them, and said,
9b   "Men, I can see that this voyage is likely to result in damage and considerable loss—not only to ship and cargo, but
even of our own lives as well."

But Julius paid more attention to the helmsman and the
captain than to Paul's words of warning. Moreover, since
the harbor is unsuitable for a ship to winter in, the majority
were in favor of setting sail again in the hope of reaching
Phoenix and wintering there. Phoenix is a harbor in Crete,
facing southwest and northwest. So, when a moderate breeze
sprang up, thinking they had obtained just what they wanted,
they weighed anchor and coasted along, hugging the shores
of Crete. But before long a terrific gale, which they called
a northeaster, swept down upon us from the land. The ship
was caught by it and since she could not be brought up into
the wind we had to let her fall off and run before it. Then,
running under the lee of a small island called Clauda, we
managed with some difficulty to secure the ship's boat. After
hoisting it aboard they used cables to brace the ship. To add

* See Map 4, page 80.

to the difficulties they were afraid all the time of drifting on
to the Syrtis banks, so they shortened sail and lay to, drifting.
The next day, as we were still at the mercy of the violent
storm, they began to throw cargo overboard. On the third
day with their own hands they threw the ship's tackle over
the side. Then, when for many days there was no glimpse of
sun or stars and we were still in the grip of the gale, all
hope of our being saved was given up.

PAUL'S PRACTICAL COURAGE AND FAITH

Nobody had eaten for some time, when Paul came for-   27
ward among the men and said,   21
"Men, you should have listened to me and not set sail
from Crete and suffered this damage and loss. However,
now I beg you to keep up your spirits for no one's life is
going to be lost, though we shall lose the ship. I know this
because last night, the angel of God to Whom I belong, and
Whom I serve, stood by me and said, 'Have no fear, Paul!
You must stand before Caesar. And God, as a mark of His
favor towards you, has granted you the lives of those who are
sailing with you.' Take courage then, men, for I believe God,
and I am certain that everything will happen exactly as I
have been told. But we shall have to run the ship ashore on
some island."

AT LAST WE NEAR LAND

On the fourteenth night of the storm, as we were drifting   27
in the Adriatic, about midnight the sailors sensed that we   27
were nearing land. Indeed, when they sounded they found
twenty fathoms, and then after sailing on only a little way
they sounded again and found fifteen. So, for fear that we
might be hurled on the rocks, they threw out four anchors
from the stern and prayed for daylight. The sailors wanted
to desert the ship and they got as far as letting a boat down
into the sea, pretending that they were going to run out
anchors from the bow. But Paul said to the centurion and the
soldiers,
"Unless these men stay aboard the ship there is no hope
of your being saved."
At this the soldiers cut the ropes of the boat and let her fall
away.

PAUL'S STURDY COMMON SENSE

27   Then while everyone waited for the day to break Paul
33 urged them to take some food, saying,

"For two weeks now you've had no food—you haven't
had a bite while you've been on watch. Now take some food,
I beg you—you need it for your own well-being, for not a
hair of anyone's head will be lost."

When he had said this he took some bread and, after thanking God before them all, he broke it and began to eat. This
raised everybody's spirits and they began to take food themselves. There were about two hundred and seventy-six of
us all told aboard that ship. When they had eaten enough
they lightened the ship by throwing the grain over the side.

LAND AT LAST—BUT WE LOSE THE SHIP

27   When daylight came no one recognized the land. But
39 they made out a bay with a sandy shore where they planned
to beach the ship if they could. So they cut away the anchors
and left them in the sea, and at the same time cut the ropes
which held the steering oars. Then they hoisted the foresail
to catch the wind and made for the beach. But they struck a
shoal and the ship ran aground. The bow stuck fast, while the
stern began to break up under the strain. The soldiers' plan
had been to kill the prisoners in case any of them should try
to swim to shore and escape. But the centurion, in his desire
to save Paul, put a stop to this, and gave orders that all those
who could swim should jump overboard first and get to land,
while the rest should follow, some on planks and others on
the wreckage of the ship. So it came true that everyone
reached the shore in safety.

A SMALL INCIDENT ESTABLISHES PAUL'S REPUTATION

28   After our escape we discovered that the island was called
1 Melita. The natives treated us with uncommon kindness.
Because of the driving rain and the cold they lit a fire and
made us all welcome. Then when Paul had collected a large
bundle of sticks and was about to put it on the fire, a viper
driven out by the heat fastened itself on his hand. When the
natives saw the creature hanging from his hand they said to
each other, "This man is obviously a murderer. He has

escaped from the sea but justice will not let him live." But Paul shook off the viper into the fire without suffering any ill effect. Naturally they expected him to swell up or suddenly fall down dead, but after waiting a long time and seeing nothing untoward happen to him, they changed their minds and kept saying that he was a god.

PAUL'S ACTS OF HEALING: THE ISLANDERS' GRATITUDE

In that part of the island were estates belonging to the governor, whose name was Publius. This man welcomed us and entertained us most kindly for three days. Now it happened that Publius' father was lying ill with fever and dysentery. Paul visited him and after prayer laid his hands on him and healed him. After that all the other sick people on the island came forward and were cured. Consequently they loaded us with presents, and when the time came for us to sail they provided us with everything we needed.

28

7

SPRING RETURNS AND WE RESUME OUR JOURNEY

It was no less than three months later that we set sail in an Alexandrian ship which had wintered in the island, a ship that had the Heavenly Twins as her figurehead. We put in at Syracuse and stayed there three days, and from there we tacked round to Rhegium. A day later the south wind sprang up and we sailed to Puteoli, reaching it in only two days. There we found some of the brothers and they begged us to stay a week with them, and so we finally came to Rome.

28

11

A CHRISTIAN WELCOME AWAITS US IN THE CAPITAL

The brothers there had heard about us and came out from the city to meet us, as far as the Market of Appius and the Three Taverns. When Paul saw them he thanked God and his spirits rose. When we reached Rome Paul was given permission to live alone with the soldier who was guarding him.

28

15

PAUL EXPLAINS HIMSELF FRANKLY TO THE JEWS IN ROME

Three days later Paul invited the leading Jews to meet him, and when they arrived he spoke to them,

"Men and brothers, although I have done nothing against our people or the customs of our forefathers, I was handed

28

17

over to the Romans as a prisoner in Jerusalem. They examined
me and were prepared to release me, since they found me
guilty of nothing deserving the death penalty. But the attacks
of the Jews there forced me to appeal to Caesar—not that I
had any charge to make against my own nation. But it is because of this accusation of the Jews that I have asked to see
you and talk matters over with you. In actual fact it is on account of the Hope of Israel that I am here in chains."

But they replied,

"We have received no letters about you from Judaea,
nor have any of the brothers who have arrived here said anything, officially or unofficially, against you. We want to hear
you state your views, although as far as this sect is concerned
we do know that serious objections have been raised to it
everywhere."

PAUL'S EARNEST AND PROLONGED EFFORT TO WIN
HIS OWN PEOPLE FOR CHRIST

28   When they had arranged a day for him they came to his
23   lodging in great numbers. From morning till evening he explained the Kingdom of God to them, giving his personal
testimony, trying to persuade them about Jesus from the
law of Moses and the prophets. As a result several of them
were won over by his words, but others would not believe.
When they could not reach any agreement among themselves
and began to go away, Paul added as a parting shot, "How
rightly did the Holy Spirit speak through the prophet Isaiah
when he said,

Go thou unto this people, and say,
By hearing ye shall hear, and shall in no wise understand;
And seeing ye shall see, and shall in no wise perceive:
For this people's heart is waxed gross,
And their ears are dull of hearing,
And their eyes they have closed;
Lest haply they should perceive with their eyes,
And hear with their ears,
And understand with their heart,
And should turn again,
And I should heal them.

"Let it be plainly understood then that this salvation of our
God has been sent to the Gentiles, and they at least will
listen to it!"

THE LAST GLIMPSE OF PAUL . . .

So Paul stayed for two full years in his own rented apart-   28
ment welcoming all who came to see him. He proclaimed to   30
them all the Kingdom of God and gave them the teaching of
the Lord Jesus Christ with the utmost freedom and without
hindrance from anyone.

PAUL'S
JOURNEY
Nº1

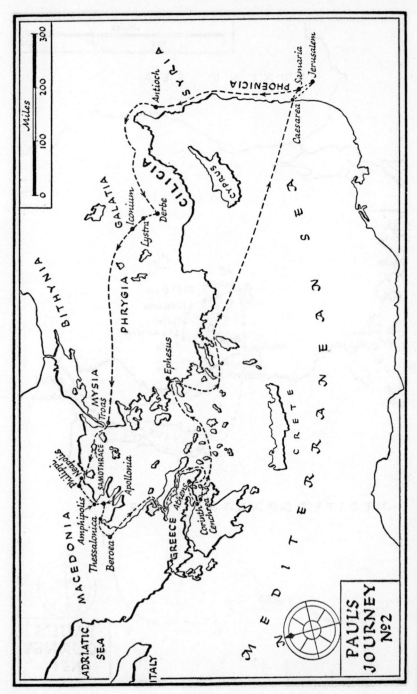

Miles
0 100 200 300

BITHYNIA

GALATIA

PHRYGIA

Iconium

Lystra

Derbe

CILICIA

SYRIA

Antioch

PHOENICIA

Samaria

Jerusalem

Caesarea

CYPRUS

MYSIA

Troas

Ephesus

Neapolis

Philippi

Amphipolis

SAMOTHRACE

Apollonia

Thessalonica

Beroea

MACEDONIA

ADRIATIC SEA

ITALY

GREECE

Athens

Corinth

Cenchrea

CRETE

MEDITERRANEAN SEA

PAUL'S JOURNEY Nº 2

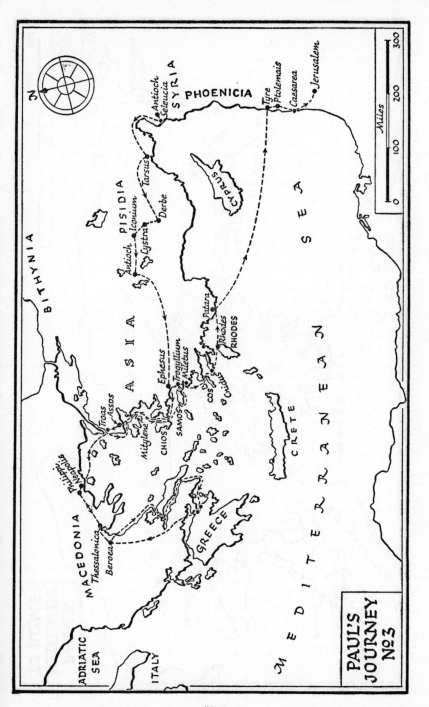

PAUL'S
JOURNEY
Nº 3

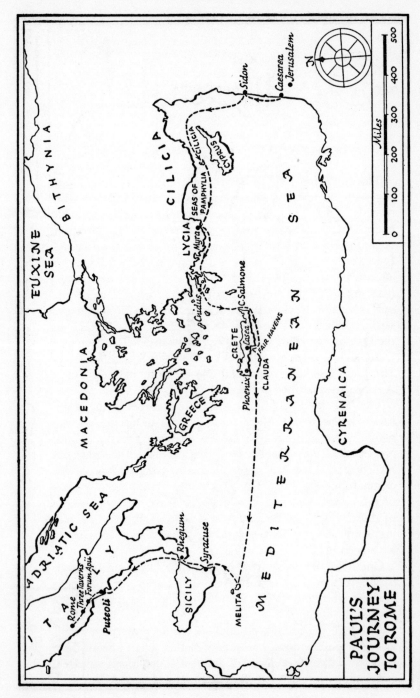

PAUL'S
JOURNEY
TO ROME

APPENDIX

The following four addresses are, as noted in the relevant pages of the text, expanded versions of what Luke actually records. These imaginative reconstructions were originally undertaken at the invitation of the Reverend E. H. Robertson, Assistant Head of Religious Broadcasting in this country. All four were broadcast on the Third Program of the B.B.C., each address being read by a professional actor. They are printed here just as they were broadcast with a "run-in" and "run-out" of a few freely translated verses to provide the proper setting, which were read by the translator. The Speech on the Day of Pentecost was read by Norman Shelley; Stephen's Defense was read by Alan Wheatley; the Speech on Mars' Hill by Carleton Hobbs, and the Defense of Paul before Agrippa by Hallam Fordham.

The fact that I ever undertook these exercises of the imagination is due to Mr. Robertson's powers of persuasion, but naturally he must not be held responsible for the results! Nevertheless, I thoroughly agree with him that the addresses recorded by Luke are almost certainly compressions of the original speeches. Luke may have worked from his own notes of the salient points of an address, or from the recollections of those who heard the words at first hand. It seems exceedingly unlikely that a verbatim report of any speech could have been made in those days.

One must therefore "read between the lines," using imagination tempered by careful study, in order to produce a credible, if hypothetical, version of what may really have been said.

Although the following addresses are no more than imaginative reconstructions, I must confess that when I heard them read by extremely competent actors I found them strangely convincing—but that may have been largely due to their skill.

J. B. P.

PETER'S SERMON ON THE DAY OF PENTECOST
(Free translation of Chapter 2) *

When the Feast of the Day of Pentecost arrived, all these
early disciples of Jesus Christ (which as I have already mentioned were about a hundred and twenty in number) had met
together in fellowship. Without the slightest warning there
came from Heaven a rushing noise like that of a tremendous
wind, and the noise filled the house in which they were sitting.
Then they saw something like fire which split off into tongues
of flame and settled over the heads of each one of them. The
Holy Spirit filled them all and they began to speak in different
languages as the Spirit moved them to proclaim His message.

Now, it happened that on this great day of the Feast of
Pentecost there were living in Jerusalem Jews of deep faith
from every nation. At the sound of this talking in various
languages a huge crowd soon collected and were completely
bewildered because every one of them found himself listening
to his own mother tongue. Astonishment and sheer wonder
spread through the crowd and some of them began to say,
"What on earth is happening? Surely all these speakers are
Galileans—how is it that every one of us is hearing the language of his own native land? Wherever we come from—
Rome, Asia, Africa, Crete, Arabia—and whether we are Jews
or proselytes, we can all hear these men speaking in our native
tongue of the great things God has done." They were completely amazed and at a loss for an explanation. "What can it
mean?" they asked one another. Some with a sneer said,
"These fellows have drunk too much new wine." Then Peter,
with the Eleven standing by him, raised his voice and spoke
to them:

"Fellow Jews and all of you who are living in Jerusalem,
there is something of the highest importance that you should
know, and I beg you to listen most carefully to my words.
These men are not drunk as some of you seem to suppose.
It is, after all, only nine o'clock on the morning of a solemn

* This address was broadcast on the Third Program of the B.B.C.,
June 29, 1954.

Feast Day! No, something tremendously important has happened. A prophecy has come true! Being Jews, as I am, you have all heard the great words of the prophet Joel, but may I remind you of some of them? Inspired by the Spirit, he wrote: 'God says that in the last days this shall happen: I will pour out my Spirit upon all flesh; your sons and your daughters shall prophesy; your young men shall see visions and your old men shall dream dreams. Upon my very servants and my handmaidens will I pour my own Spirit and they too shall prophesy.'

"This, my brothers in the faith of our fathers, is the *Word of God coming true before your eyes*. These men are prophesying. These men have seen visions and are dreaming dreams, for God's own Spirit has filled them and He is speaking through them! The prophet Joel, you will remember, went on to tell of other things that should come to pass. Speaking in the Name of God, he said, 'I will show wonders in the heaven above and signs on the earth beneath; blood and fire and vapor of smoke. The sun shall be turned into darkness and the moon into blood before the Day of the Lord come, that great and radiant Day.' Now we have not yet seen the sun turned into darkness or the moon into blood, and the last great glorious Day of the Lord has not yet come, though not one of us can tell how near or how far that Day may be. But today, on this Feast of Pentecost, before your astonished eyes the first part of that great prophecy has been mightily fulfilled.

"Therefore, men of Israel, I beg you, pay close attention to what I have to say now.

"A Man lived among you here in our own country, and indeed was often in this city, Whom God plainly showed to be His Own by great deeds, by miracles and many signs for those with eyes to see. His Name was Jesus of Nazareth, and to you who have come here from far away, I have to tell you that we knew this Man, we heard His marvelous teaching and saw His wonderful works. In our very streets and homes, upon our hills and by our lakesides, in villages and towns, as well as here in Jerusalem itself, He spoke such words as no man has ever spoken and God worked through Him many mighty miracles. Some of you, like me, will never forget how He cleansed the lepers; how at a word of command from Him devils would come out of a man or woman or child. Were we all blind not to see Who this was Who lived and worked and moved among us? If I close my eyes I can see Him now in a house crowded with people, and then the daylight breaking through from above as four men in their desperation to bring their paralyzed friend to Jesus, let him down through the broken roof. 'My son,' said this Jesus to the man who lay there quite helpless, 'your sins are forgiven you, pick up your bed and walk!' Never shall I forget the astonished faces as this man did indeed do what Jesus commanded him. Yes, there were plenty to murmur, 'Who is this man who dares to forgive sins, which God alone can do?' Yet Jesus made this not only the proof of His power but the proof that He was indeed the Chosen One of God. The man rose and walked, and walks to this day. And then I think of a man totally blind whom Jesus made to see, at first not perfectly, for well we remember his strange remark, 'I can see men but they're like trees walking about.' Then Jesus touched him again and he saw sharp and clear, and is seeing to this day. Some of my friends here were with me when we saw Jesus, at the height of the storm, command the raging waves of the lake to be still, and they obeyed him. We can remember Him bringing back to life a little girl of twelve, we can remember how a woman in the crowd had only to touch Him to be healed of a disease that had caused her years of misery. So much can we remember and so ashamed are we that we were so slow and blind to recognize Him for the One He really was!

"In spite of all these wonders and miracles, in spite of the words which rang with the authority of God, we were fearful and slow to believe. He knew what was to happen, yet He set His face steadfastly to come here to Jerusalem, knowing that it would mean His certain death. At the end it was our Chief Priests and elders who conspired to have him crucified, yet it was one of us who betrayed Him that night in the garden. We all ran for our lives, and I myself in fear for my own safety denied three times that I had ever known Him.

"Yes, by you the Chosen People of God, the Chosen Son of God was handed over to Gentiles and crucified like any common criminal. He, the Christ of God, suffered every possible indignity. They jeered at Him, they slapped Him and they flogged Him and in the end they nailed Him to a cross of wood. Yes, you the Jewish people did this to God's Chosen One. Yet neither our blindness, our wickedness nor our fear could defeat God's foreknowledge and God's already determined Plan. This Jesus Whom you murdered God raised up, never allowing the bitter pains of death to touch Him; indeed, there was nothing by which death could hold such a Man.

"Now, fellow Jews, we all know that in our Scriptures holy men of old spoke as they were moved by the very Spirit of God. I have already mentioned the prophecy of Joel, but here I want to bring back to your minds some words of our great forefather David, in which I am convinced he was writing of this same Jesus, the Christ of God. He wrote: 'I saw the Lord always before my face, for He is on my right hand that I should not be moved. Therefore, my heart was glad and my tongue rejoiced.' So far you may say you understand the words of David. They are words of trust and confidence in God and they are not of necessity a prophecy. But recollect how David continues, 'Moreover my flesh shall rest in hope because thou wilt not leave my soul in Hades, neither wilt thou let thine Holy One see corruption. Thou hast made known to me the paths of life and thou wilt make me delight in thy Presence.'

"Now, my brothers, let me speak to you with the utmost candor. David is one of our most highly honored patriarchs, but he could not have been writing of himself when he spoke of the Holy One Who should not see corruption; for he himself both died and was buried and his tomb is with us to this very day. Now David was not only a king and a sweet singer of psalms, *he was a prophet*. He knew that God had promised him with a most solemn oath that He would put one of his descendants upon His throne. As a prophet he took this not literally, as some might suppose, but he foresaw the Resurrection of the Christ, and it is of Him that he is speaking here. For Christ was not left to the mercy of death and His body was never destroyed. I say to you now that that Christ is Jesus of Nazareth, Whom God Himself raised from the dead, and all of you standing with me here are eyewitnesses to the fact that He was in truth raised from the dead. Now

He has been exalted to God's right hand and has poured upon us who know and love Him the promised Holy Spirit which He has received from the Father. This outpouring is what you are seeing and hearing at this very moment.

"David great man though he was, never ascended to Heaven, but he said, 'The Lord said to my Lord: Sit thou at my right hand till I make thine enemies thy footstool.' What is the meaning of this mysterious sentence? What 'Lord' is David referring to, whom the Lord God is commanding to sit at His own right hand until his enemies were made his footstool? Surely he is prophesying of the Holy One, the Christ, the One Who should not see corruption, even though He were put to death? Can you not see that David with the insight of a prophet was foreseeing his own Lord and ours, this very Man Jesus, the Christ of God, Whom God would not permit death to hold, and Whom God has now raised to the highest place of power? My brothers, the whole household of Israel must now know beyond a shadow of doubt that this Jesus Whom you crucified God has made both 'Lord' and 'Christ.'"

These words of Peter's went through their hearts like a sword, and they exclaimed to Peter and the other disciples, "You are Jews as we are, what can we do now?" Peter replied, "The answer is simple. You must repent and each one of you must be baptized in the Name of this same Jesus Christ that your sins may be forgiven. Then this outpouring of the Spirit, all this strength and courage and joy that has come to us will come to you as well. For the promise prophesied by the prophet Joel is meant for you and your children, and for all of us however far away we may be at this moment, for everyone whom the Lord our God shall call to Himself!"

These words are only a brief record of what Peter said, for in actual fact he made appeal after appeal to the people and urged them with the utmost earnestness, crying, "Save yourselves from this perverted generation." So those who welcomed his message were baptized and on that day alone about three thousand souls were added to the number of the disciples. They listened to the Apostles with the closest attention and joined them in their fellowship, in their common breaking of bread and in their prayers.

STEPHEN'S SERMON
(Free translation of Chapters 6 and 7) *

About this time, when the number of disciples was increasing, the Greeks complained that in the daily distribution of food the Hebrew widows were being given preferential treatment. The Twelve summoned the whole body of the disciples together and spoke to them:

"It is not right that we should have to give up preaching the Word of God in order to look after the accounts. You, our brothers, must look round and find from your number seven men of good repute who are both practical and full of the Spirit, and we will put them in charge of this matter. Then we shall devote ourselves wholeheartedly to prayer and the ministry of God's Word."

This brief speech met with unanimous approval and they chose Stephen, a man full of faith and the Holy Spirit, and six others. These men were brought before the Apostles who, after prayer, laid their hands upon them.

So the Word of God continued to expand. The number of disciples in Jerusalem increased very greatly while a considerable proportion of the priesthood accepted the Faith.

Stephen, full of grace and spiritual power, was performing miracles and remarkable signs among the people. However, some members of a Jewish synagogue known as the Libertines, and some from the synagogues of Cyrene and Alexandria, and of Cilicia and Asia, attempted to dispute with Stephen, but they found themselves quite unable to stand up against the practical wisdom of his words. Whereupon they bribed men to allege, "We have heard this man making blasphemous statements against Moses and against God." They worked on the feelings of the people, the elders and the scribes. Then they suddenly confronted Stephen, seized him and marched him off before the Sanhedrin. There they put up false witnesses to say, "This man's speeches are one long attack directed against this holy place and the Law. For we have heard him say that this Jesus of Nazareth will destroy

* This address was broadcast on the Third Program of the B.B.C., Dec. 26, 1954.

this place and change the customs which Moses gave us." All who sat there in the Sanhedrin looked intently at Stephen, and as they looked his face appeared to them like the face of an angel.

Then the High Priest asked him: "Is this statement true?" And Stephen answered:

"My brothers and my fathers, I ask you to listen to me. We all know how our glorious God appeared to Abraham in Mesopotamia, before he ever lived in Haran, and we all remember God's words to him which were, 'Get thee out of thy land and from thy kindred, and come into the land which I shall show thee.' Abraham heard God's Voice and he obeyed it. He left the land of the Chaldeans and went to live in Haran, and it was from there after the death of his father that he was moved, again at God's command, into this very land where we are living today. Abraham indeed obeyed God in faith, for he was not given a foot of this land to call his own. All he was given was a promise—a promise that one day the land should belong to him and to his descendants—and this at a time when he had no descendant at all!

"It was truly a strange promise that God gave to Abraham. He was told that for four hundred years his descendants should live as strangers in a strange land and would be ill treated as slaves. Yet there was future light in that Promise, for God also told Abraham that after the four hundred years were passed He Himself would judge the people who had become their masters, so that they themselves might come out from that land and serve Him here in this country.

"Now Abraham believed that Promise, strange though it was, and later when the Solemn Agreement was marked by that unforgettable rite of circumcision, he never faltered, but circumcised Isaac, his first-born son. Abraham was surely a shining example to us of a man who believed God in absolute faith in almost impossible circumstances.

"So, brothers and fathers, as you all know, the years went by. After Abraham came Isaac, and then Jacob and the twelve patriarchs. Yes, we call them the twelve patriarchs, but let that not blind us to the fact that they fell far below the sublime faith of Abraham. Indeed, it was through common jealousy and spite that they sold Joseph their own brother as a slave into Egypt. Yet you all know well that the failure of man cannot defeat the Purpose of God, and God never forgot His Promise. Although Joseph was living in a strange and heathen land, God was always with him to deliver him out of all his troubles and make him a man both trusted and respected in the eyes of Pharaoh the king of Egypt.

"Then came the famine over all the land of Egypt and Canaan which caused great suffering. But again we can see how the hand of God works whatever the circumstances of men. You can see the strange irony which sent the patriarchs, under the stress of famine, back to Joseph whom they had sold as a slave, since they had heard that there was 'corn in Egypt.' It was only on their second visit that Joseph let them know who he was and Pharaoh realized from what race Joseph had sprung. For the time all went well, as Joseph invited all his kinsmen, some seventy-five in all, to come and live with him in Egypt.

"In course of time Jacob and the patriarchs died and their bodies were carried for burial into the only little piece of land which Abraham really owned, for all the great promises that were made to him—that part of Shechem which he had had to buy with silver from the sons of Hamor, Shechem's father.

"Again, time went on and the four hundred years in God's Promise had nearly elapsed. Naturally our people had grown more and more numerous in the land of Egypt, but there came to the throne a king who knew nothing about Joseph. He used great cunning in exploiting our people, and he even forced them to expose their infant children so that our race might die out. This must indeed have looked like the defeat of God's purpose. Yet it was at this very time that Moses was born—a child of such remarkable beauty that, when the time came for him to be abandoned, Pharaoh's daughter adopted him and brought him up as her own son. So while our forefathers toiled and suffered as slaves, Moses was trained in all the wisdom of Egypt. He became a speaker of great power and a man of action as well.

"Then, when this outstanding man Moses had reached the age of forty, he thought he should go and observe how the Israelites, his own brothers, were faring. It happened that he saw one of them being unjustly treated and went at once to his rescue, striking down the Egyptian who was ill treating his brother. He thought and hoped that all his brothers would understand by this action that God was bringing salvation to them at his hands. But they completely failed to perceive that God had raised up such a man to rescue them. The very next day he came across some of them who were quarreling and remonstrated with them in the words, 'You are brothers of the same race; what good can you do by quarreling with one another?' The man who had picked the quarrel pushed his neighbor aside and flared at Moses, 'Who made you a ruler and judge over us? Do you want to kill me as you killed that Egyptian yesterday?' This utter lack of understanding of what he was trying to do, and of what he could do, for his own people so horrified and unnerved Moses that he ran away from Egypt altogether, and for forty years lived as a stranger in the land of Midian where he became the father of two sons. I hope we can all understand this action of Moses. We do not know, but surely we can reasonably suppose that, although he was brought up among the Egyptians, he never forgot to what race he belonged and that there came to him a growing conviction that God had chosen him and trained him to come to the rescue of his own people. Yet when he went to their rescue he was met with such misjudgment, such blindness, such utter rejection of himself as the one whom God had sent, that he recoiled in bitter disappointment.

"So it was forty years later, in the desert of Mount Sinai, that an angel of the Lord appeared to him in the burning bush. The vision filled Moses with wonder, and as he approached to look at it more closely the Voice of the Lord Himself spoke to him: 'I am the God of thy fathers, the God of Abraham, and of Isaac, and of Jacob.' Then Moses, great and able man that he was, trembled and was afraid to look any closer, but the Lord spoke to him again and said, 'Put off thy shoes from thy feet: for the place whereon thou standest is holy ground. I have surely seen the affliction of my people which is in Egypt, and have heard their groaning, and I am come down to deliver them: and now come, I will send thee into Egypt.' So, and notice this well, this same Moses, whom the people of Israel had rejected in the contemptuous words, 'Who made you a ruler and a judge over us?' God sent to be both their ruler and their savior. Yes, this man whom the people of Israel had rejected was in fact to become their savior, for he led them out of the land of Egypt showing them both there and when they crossed the Red Sea unmistakable signs that the power of God was with him.

"For forty years he was their leader in the desert and he was the man who on Mount Sinai stood between the angel and our people and received words which are still living words and which have been handed down to you today. He was the man who said to our forefathers, 'God shall raise up from among you a prophet such as I am.' Yet this was also the man whom our forefathers refused to listen to. They turned aside from him; in their hearts they hankered after the safety of Egypt. For even while Moses was receiving the very Law of God on the mountain, they called to Aaron and said, 'Make us gods that we can see to go before us, for as for this man Moses who led us out of Egypt, we do not know what has happened to him.' So they began to worship the calf of gold and even offered a sacrifice to their idol. And they rejoiced in the work of their own hands. And what was the result of this blindness, this failure to see the one whom God had sent to be their leader? This, that God Himself turned away from them and left them to worship other gods. And they took up the tabernacle of Moloch, and worshiped the figures which they themselves had made.

"Yet during all those years in the desert our forefathers possessed the Tabernacle of Witness made according to the pattern which God Himself gave to Moses when He commanded him to make it. This same tabernacle was handed on by our forefathers. And when the man arrived who drove out the Gentiles from this land by the power of God, whose name I would remind you was Jesus, this same tabernacle was still with them and stayed in this our land until the time of David. David, a man after God's own heart, won the approval of our glorious God and prayed earnestly that he might find a habitation for the God of Jacob, even though it was not he but his son Solomon who built a house for the Most High. But as we all know the God Whom we worship does not live in temples made by man. As the prophet says, 'The heaven is my throne, and the earth the footstool of my feet: what manner of house will ye build Me? saith the Lord: or what is the place of my rest? Did not my hand make all these things?'

"Surely the lesson we can learn is that it is neither tabernacle nor temple but God Himself Who is all-important. Men
can have a tabernacle or a temple in their very midst and yet
fail to recognize the man whom God has chosen when he
appears. I am accused of speaking against both Law and
Temple; I do neither. But I must and will speak against this
continual blindness, this continual refusal to recognize God's
Living Servant.

"Think back, men and brothers, over the centuries of which
I have just reminded you! Think of that well nigh incredible
faith of Abraham to whom the Promise was first given. Have
any of you shown faith in the promises of God such as that?
Think of Moses raised up by God in the strangest way to
rescue God's own people, and yet how those same people
rejected him with contempt. Is there one among you who has
not shown the same blindness to the strange ways of God's
working, the same unwillingness to follow and obey the One
Whom God has chosen? I suggest to you it was no mere acci-
dent that the man who led our people into this land, the leader
appointed by God and empowered by God, was named—
Jesus.

"Am I not justified in calling you obstinate, Godless in your
thinking, yes, Godless in the very way you are listening to
me now! It is always the same—you men of Israel never fail
to resist the Holy Spirit. Just as your fathers acted so have
you acted now. Can you name a single prophet whom your
fathers did not persecute? They killed the men who foretold
the coming of the Righteous One, the Jesus of our day. And
now you have become His betrayers and His murderers. You
are the men who have received the very Law of God miraculously, by the hand of angels, *and you are the men who have
disobeyed it.*"

When they heard that they were cut to the heart and
ground their teeth at him in rage.

Stephen, filled through all his being with the Holy Spirit,
looked steadily up into Heaven. He saw the glory of God,
and Jesus Himself standing at His right hand. "Look!" he
exclaimed, "the heavens are opened and I can see the Son of
Man standing at God's right hand!" At this, they put their
fingers in their ears. Yelling with fury, as one man they made

a rush at him and hustled him out of the city, and stoned him. The witnesses of the execution left their outer garments at the feet of a young man whose name was Saul.

So they stoned Stephen while he called upon God and said, "Jesus, Lord, receive my spirit!" Then, on his knees, he cried in ringing tones, "Lord, forgive them for this sin." And with these words he fell into the sleep of death.

Meanwhile Saul gave silent assent to his execution.

PAUL'S SERMON ON MARS' HILL
(Free translation of Chapter 17) *

Paul had some days to wait at Athens for Silas and Timothy to arrive, and while he was there his soul was exasperated beyond endurance at the sight of a city so completely idolatrous. He felt compelled to discuss the matter first in the Synagogue with the Jews, then with the proselytes that he found there, and he even argued daily in the open market place with the passers-by. While he was speaking there some Epicurean and Stoic philosophers came across him and some of them remarked, "What is this cock sparrow trying to say?" Others said, "He seems to be trying to proclaim some more gods to us, and outlandish ones at that!" For Paul was actually proclaiming Jesus and the Resurrection. So quite good-humoredly they got hold of him, and conducted him to their Council, the Areopagus. There they asked him, "May we know what this new teaching of yours really is? You talk of matters which sound strange to our ears, and we should like to know what they mean." (Now this desire for explanation can only be understood if we realize that the Athenians, and even foreign visitors to Athens, had an obsession for any novelty, and would spend their whole time listening to or talking about anything that was new.) So Paul got to his feet in the middle of their Council and began:

"Gentlemen of Athens, I am very glad of this opportunity of speaking to you, even though it has been somewhat thrust

* This address was broadcast on the Third Program of the B.B.C., Oct. 18, 1953.

upon me! For since my arrival a few days ago, I have been, not to put too fine a point on it, profoundly shocked by the vast number of images which I see set up all over your city. The reason for this large number of shrines and idols I have already discussed during the last few days with my fellow Jews in the synagogues, and with other religious people. Indeed, I have even spoken of the matter in your market place day after day. Now that you have asked me to speak to you almost as it were officially in this distinguished gathering, I will at least say this, that you are evidently an extremely religious people. I have seen evidence of this everywhere, and even on my way here I noticed all kinds of shrines dedicated to the worship of all sorts of gods. But there was one particular altar which caught my eye, which was inscribed quite simply, 'To God the Unknown.' Yes, someone inscribed it 'To God the Unknown,' the one true God of Whom on your own admission you know nothing, for all your shrines and statues . . . and yet it is this God, unknown to you but, by His great mercy, known to me, Whom I have the honor now to stand and proclaim to you!

"God, the true God, is far greater than you suppose. He is the God above all gods, the King above all kings, the Lord above all lords. He is the Creator and Sustainer of this whole world and everything contained in it, great or small. It is by His power and permission that Heaven and earth exist and nothing, either great or small, lies beyond His sovereign power. Now how, gentlemen of Athens, how can the true God, the Creator of all and the Power behind both Heaven and earth, be thought to live in a man-made shrine? How can you imagine for one moment that creatures of human clay could in the slightest degree minister to His needs! For, after all, what could He need when everything belongs to Him? Could a man give anything to Him Who alone gives life and breath and everything else to all mankind? For God, the true God, Who made all things, made also, in His own image, man.

"Yes, of His own will He made man in His own image, thus conferring on him unspeakable honor. (But surely you will see that it is no honor to God that man should attempt to make the Uncreated One in man's image!) And from this first man whom God created from the dust of the earth He has peopled the world. He has made all nations of men who live on this earth, and it is by His will that the very times of their existence are determined; it is by His will that the countries which they inhabit are also appointed.

"Now why should such a God be 'God the Unknown' to you? It seems to me that God has left Himself in all His creation a witness to His own greatness and power, and it also seems to me that He has set in the hearts of all men the desire to feel after Him and find Him. The gods of all nations, your very gods themselves, testify to the fact that men everywhere are groping for the one true God. Yes, though as a worshiper of the true God I have been shocked by all your idols, yet are not these idols themselves witnesses that God has implanted in the hearts of men the desire to worship Him? Gods who are not true gods I have found in many nations, yet they serve to show the desire of mankind to seek for and worship the one true God. You are not alone in the hope that you will one day find Him.

"No one has seen God at any time and there are many who have not known Him, yet in fact He is not far away from any one of us. He is the One Who is all about us and we can say in perfect truth that it is 'in Him we live and move and have our being.' Indeed, I remember that your own poets have said, 'We too are His children.'

"Now, gentlemen of Athens, I know that you are quick to ridicule the absurd and I know that foolish thinking strikes you as such as soon as any man. Can you not see the absurdity of supposing that, if we are children of the most high God, we should for one moment imagine Him to be like the silver or gold or stone images which human art or imagination has contrived! Why, in your own philosophies there are thoughts and ideas far above the empty worshiping of idols, which cannot possibly satisfy the needs of the hearts of men. If God be God, the supreme Creator, the Source of all wisdom and goodness and truth, He is as far above these paltry images as the Heaven is high above the earth.

"Now in past ages God has in truth not shown Himself plainly. Of His own set purpose He has kept hidden until these last days the mystery of how He would make Himself known to men. I am convinced that while men were in the dark, God overlooked their blindness and their stupidities. But now the picture is changed, now God has spoken! Now He commands men everywhere to repent, not merely to be sorry for the evil things they have done, but to change their whole outlook to conform to His great and glorious Plan. Now He has appointed a Day in which He will judge all men justly. He has declared that the standard by which He will judge the world will be, not their own ideas, nor even their own conscience, but the standard of a living Man by Whose Life the lives of all men will be shown for what they are. In solemn truth I tell you that all men will stand before the judgment seat of this Man and give account of what they did while they lived this life, whether that were good or bad.

"Prophets and seers of old had many glimpses of the truth, but now in these latter days God has given us the Truth itself in one Man Whom He has destined to be the living Truth. He is God's Son, the radiance of the glory of God, the flawless Expression of the Nature of God shown in a human being. He is the One through Whom we know God the Unknown. For it is in this Man that God has chosen to reveal Himself, and not only to reveal Himself, but to reconcile to Himself all men who will put their trust in the One Whom He has chosen.

"But someone of course will say, 'What is the proof of this? How can we know that this Man is truly what He claimed to be, and has truly shown to us the Nature and the Plan of God?' I will tell you quite simply. Only a few years ago evil men plotted against that Man. Their darkness could not bear His light and in their furious desire to quench His light they put Him to death, the death of a common criminal. But, and here is your proof, and the proof to all men, God Himself raised that Man from the dead, and He is alive today!"

But when his audience heard Paul talk about a Man being raised from the dead, some of them laughed outright, but there were others who said, "We should like to hear you speak again on this subject." So Paul retired from their assembly, his speech having apparently made little impression. Yet some did in fact join him later and accept the Faith, including a member of the Areopagus by the name of Dionysius, a woman called Damaris, and others as well. But before long Paul left Athens altogether and went on to Corinth.

PAUL'S SPEECH BEFORE AGRIPPA
(Free translation of Chapter 26) *

[Before Paul's famous speech to Agrippa he had been kept
in custody for over two years. The trouble had arisen when
Paul made a journey of about sixty miles from Caesarea on
the coast of Palestine to Jerusalem, which he had not visited
for several years. Very naturally he entered the Temple, but
a number of fanatical Jews who were bitterly opposed to
Paul's Christian Gospel stirred up the mob, dragged him out
and very nearly succeeded in beating him to death. The Roman authorities intervened, however, and he was saved from
a flogging at their hands by revealing the fact that he was
born a citizen of Rome. He was then given the opportunity
of addressing the Sanhedrin, the Jews' Supreme Council, but
there his claim to be a Pharisee and his insistence on the
Resurrection turned a normally august assembly into a
murderous mob. Once again he was rescued by the Roman
authorities, and shortly afterwards had to appear before Felix
the Roman procurator as being the ringleader of the insur-
rection of the sect called Nazarenes. He denied this particular
charge and pointed out that he was a follower of the Way
of Jesus Christ and firmly believed in the Resurrection. Felix
knew something about the Christian way of life, and for the
time being remanded Paul in custody, and in view of his being
a Roman citizen ordered him to be given favorable treatment.
This custody went on for many months, during which time
Felix had several conversations with Paul. The latter was still
held prisoner when Nero recalled Felix to Rome and appointed Festus as Governor in his place.]

Some days later King Agrippa and Bernice arrived at
Caesarea on a State visit to Festus the Governor. They prolonged their stay for several days, and this gave Festus an
opportunity of putting Paul's case before the King.

"I have a man here," he said, "who was imprisoned by my
predecessor, Felix. Last time I was at Jerusalem the Chief

* This address was broadcast on the Third Program of the B.B.C.,
Jan. 25, 1954.

Priests and Elders of the Jews presented their case against him, and pretty well demanded his conviction. I told them that Romans were not in the habit of convicting anybody until he had had the chance of facing his accusers personally, and had been given the opportunity of defending himself on the charges made against him. When they heard this these Jews came back here with me. I wasted no time, but on the very next day I took my seat on the Bench and ordered the man to be brought in. But when his accusers got up to speak they did not charge him with any such crimes as I had anticipated. Their differences with him lay purely in the realm of religion, and were about a man called Jesus Who had died, but Who, Paul maintained, was still alive. Frankly, I did not feel qualified to investigate such matters, and so I asked the man if he was willing to go to Jerusalem and stand his trial there. But Paul appealed to have his case laid before the Emperor himself. So I have kept him in custody here until I find an opportunity to send him to the Emperor."

"I should very much like to hear the man myself," said Agrippa.

"You shall hear him tomorrow," replied Festus.

So next day Agrippa and Bernice proceeded to the audience chamber with great pomp and ceremony, with an escort of military officers and prominent townsmen. Then Festus ordered Paul to be brought in.

"King Agrippa and all of you who are present," said Festus, "you see here the man about whom the whole Jewish people both at Jerusalem and in this city have petitioned me. They insist that he should die, but I have discovered nothing that he has done which deserves the death penalty. Moreover, since he has appealed to Caesar, I have decided to send him to Rome. Nevertheless, I have nothing definite to write to our Emperor in the letter which will go with him, and I have, therefore, had him brought before you all, and especially before you, King Agrippa. I hope that from your examination of him there will emerge some definite charge which I can put in writing. For, to be frank, it seems to me a ridiculous thing to send a prisoner before the Emperor without being able to indicate definite charges against him."

Then Agrippa said to Paul, "You have our permission to speak for yourself."

So Paul with a characteristic gesture of the hand began his defense.

"King Agrippa, in answering all the charges that the Jews have made against me, I must begin by saying how fortunate I consider myself in making my defense before you personally today. I say this not to flatter you, but because I know that through your own training and circumstances you are thoroughly familiar with our religion. You know our observances and customs and you are well acquainted with our problems and disputes. It is therefore with confidence that I ask you to listen patiently while I state my case.

"As you know, I was born at Tarsus and I am therefore a Roman citizen, but I was brought up and educated as a Jew and that is no secret from anybody. My whole life since I came to Jerusalem is an open book to any Jew who cares to look into it. I don't wish to boast of my own importance, but surely any Jew who has taken the trouble to make any enquiry about me at all knows that I lived for years as a Pharisee—I kept most scrupulously the strictest principles of our religion. If they are implying that I am somehow not a proper Jew, I can say without boasting that no man is more of a Jew than I. I am sprung from the stock of Israel, a Hebrew of the Hebrews, one of the Tribe of Benjamin, and I am proud of it!

"Now the irony of the situation, King Agrippa, is this, that certain promises were made, as you know, by the Lord God to the Jews of old time, and I find myself standing on trial today because I dare to believe that those promises have been fulfilled. You will remember, Your Majesty, the prophecies of Isaiah, the prophecies in the psalms of David, and indeed throughout the Prophets, of One Who should come to rule in righteousness upon the earth. For centuries this hope has sustained our people, and to this very moment the twelve tribes pray to God unceasingly that the hope may be fulfilled. Now I dare to believe that the Messiah has come! The King has arrived. The Holy One of Israel has been present among us. *His Name is Jesus of Nazareth!* Thousands of people knew Him and heard His teaching. Yes, possibly some of you who can hear my voice today heard His voice. Thousands were healed by Him of all kinds of sickness and disease. Thousands heard Him speak with the authority of the very Son of God.

But, King Agrippa, only a few knew Who it was Who lived among them. Only a few believed in Him. As for our leaders, they hated Him with bitter hatred, for they could not see in Him the fulfillment of God's Promise—they could only see the crowning wickedness of a Man claiming to be the Son of God. Yet, even in their fury, they could find nothing wrong, no single fault in that Perfect Life, only the crime of claiming to be what He really was, the Christ of God. So, as you well know, they had Him crucified, but He was no mere man. He was not like the Prophets whom, God forgive us, my people have so often ill treated and slain. He was God's Son, and, as a triumphant justification of His claims and as a re-sounding demonstration of His own power, God raised Him from the dead. That is what I believe, that is what I know to be true. And that, King Agrippa, is what sticks in their throats, that God raised that Man from the dead. Is it that they doubt the power of God to raise His own Son from the dead, or is it that if they admit such a thing they will be condemning themselves for their own wickedness in putting Him to death?

"Now what they are feeling, I have felt also. I too was angry, furiously angry, at the blasphemy. I too stood to destroy the cause of this Man, Jesus of Nazareth. I not only felt it my duty to do all that lay in my power to stamp out this hideous blasphemy, but in actual fact, that is what I did in Jerusalem, backed with the authority of my own Chief Priests. It was through me that many Christians were imprisoned, and when they stood on trial for their lives, I voted without hesitation for their death. Again and again, I had them punished in the synagogues. I used every means to force them to curse their own Lord. I was mad with fury against them; I hounded them from pillar to post. I gave them no peace. They were never safe for a moment when I was on their trail. And if I didn't have them imprisoned, I used to hound them out of their homes, until they fled to distant cities.

"It was in this frame of mind, King Agrippa, that I was one day making my way to Damascus. I was armed with the full authority and definite commission of the Chief Priests to do what I could to uproot and destroy the following of this Man Jesus. On that journey, Your Majesty, in the full glare of mid-day, I suddenly saw a light far brighter than the sun blaze around me and my fellow travelers. Every one of us fell to the ground, and while I was lying there in the dust I heard a Voice speaking to me in my own language which said, 'Saul, Saul, why are you persecuting Me? It is not easy for you to kick against your own conscience.' 'Who are you, Sir?' I faltered. *'I am Jesus Whom you are persecuting,'* was the Lord's reply. Then He went on, 'Now get up and stand on your feet, for I show Myself to you for a particular purpose. From now on you will be My servant. You will be a witness to what you have seen this day, and to other visions which I will give you. I will keep you safe from your own people'—and then, judge of my amazement when He added—'and from the Gentiles to whom I am sending you!' I could hardly believe my ears. Yet here was undoubtedly the Christ of God telling me in person that He was sending me, a Jew, to work for Him among Gentiles, pagans, idolators, and worse. Then the Voice went on, 'I am sending you to open their eyes, to turn them from darkness to light, from the power of Satan to the power of God, so that they too may receive forgiveness of sin, and take their place with all those who are sanctified by faith in Me.'

"These words astounded me for, like all good Jews, I had always believed that the promises were made to us and to our children. Never for one moment did I imagine that the promises of the Most High could be intended for the Gentiles. I knew that this new light could never have been my imagination, and that I had in truth seen a vision. I am sure that you will understand that I could not disobey that vision from Heaven. Indeed I obeyed it promptly. In Damascus, and then in Jerusalem, and later through all the cities of Judaea I preached that all men must repent, and turn to God and live as men whose hearts are truly changed. I preached this message to both Jew and Gentile, and it was not long before God called me in a vision to preach Christ in Macedonia. I labored in many cities there, and in spite of all kinds of perils and hardships, by the grace of God I have proclaimed Christ, and salvation through his Name in many pagan cities. Corinth and Athens, Philippi and Ephesus, Antioch and Colossae are but a few of the towns where God's news of salvation has been proclaimed.

"Now ever since that vision and that Voice, King Agrippa, I have known myself commissioned by the Lord Jesus Christ

Himself to proclaim the Gospel to all men, Jew or Gentile, Greek or barbarian, slave or free man. Always I went first to the synagogue of my own people, but always it was they who became my enemies when they saw that I was determined to take the Good News to all men. Indeed, it is because I am known to be taking the fulfillment of the promise made long ago to our forefathers to every race and condition of man that the Jews arrested me in the Temple, and have even tried to kill me. There have been times, many times, when I have had to stand alone in my defense of the Gospel. Sometimes all men have forsaken me, but the Lord, according to His promise, has always stood by me, even as He stands by me today, as I bear my witness before high and low.

"I beg you to notice, King Agrippa, that in the message which I proclaim I am adding nothing to what was foretold by the prophets—I only claim that their words have been fulfilled. You will remember how in the writings of Moses there are foreshadowings of things to come—the Passover Lamb, the Serpent of brass, 'the greater Prophet,' of which he writes in the second book of the Law—all these are fulfilled in the Christ of God. Isaiah wrote of the Holy Child Who should come and bear rule over the nation, of the Servant Who should suffer for mankind's sake. Jeremiah and Zechariah both wrote of the Branch which should spring out of the stock of Jesse; all these, and many more foretellings have come true in Jesus Christ the Son of God. They knew, these Prophets, by the Holy Spirit Who moved them, that Christ should suffer and yet should ultimately triumph. And He did triumph. For to bring the glorious light both to our people and to all men everywhere God raised Him from the dead!"

While he was thus defending himself, Festus burst out:

"You are raving, Paul! All your learning and study have driven you mad."

But Paul said:

"I am not mad, Your Excellency, I speak nothing but the sober truth. These things were prophesied and these things have come true. The King knows of these matters, and I can speak freely before him. Indeed, I am sure he is well acquainted with what really happened. For the death and resurrection of Jesus was no hole-and-corner business—why, the whole of Jerusalem was ringing with it at the time! King Agrippa, do you believe that the Prophets were real prophets? But I need not ask, I know that you believe them."

"Much more of this, Paul," returned Agrippa, "and you will be making me a Christian!"

"Ah," replied Paul, "whether it means much more or only a little, I would to God that you and all who can hear me now might stand where I stand—but without these chains!"

After these words the King rose to his feet and so did the Governor and Bernice and those who were sitting with them. And when they had retired from the Assembly they discussed the matter among themselves and agreed "This man is doing nothing that deserves the death sentence." Agrippa remarked to Festus,

"We might easily have set this man free if he had not appealed to Caesar."